ALL · IN · ONE

AWS Certified Cloud Practitioner

EXAM GUIDE

(Exam CLF-C01)

ABOUT THE AUTHOR

Daniel Carter, AWS CCP, CISSP, CCSP, CISM, CISA, is a senior systems engineer with Johns Hopkins University & Medicine. An IT security and systems professional for almost 25 years, he has worked extensively with web-based applications and infrastructure, as well as LDAP, SAML, and federated identity systems; PKI; SIEM; and Linux/Unix systems. Daniel holds a degree in criminology and criminal justice from the University of Maryland and a master's degree in technology management, with a focus on homeland security management, from the University of Maryland Global Campus.

About the Technical Editor

Taylor York is a cloud application architect at Amazon Web Services, where he assists customers in designing cloud-native applications with a focus on developer satisfaction, fast cycle times, testability, and automation.

Taylor has quite the diverse background, which includes testing jet engines for the U.S. Air Force, based in Oklahoma City, Oklahoma, as well as test strategy and test architecture of mainframe and cloud applications. Most recently his efforts have been on big data and enterprise web applications on AWS.

Taylor has a wide variety of interests outside of work. He loves working on cars, watching movies, and traveling and is a definite sports enthusiast. He always enjoys cheering on his Oklahoma State Cowboys regardless of the sport. Taylor resides in Southlake, Texas, with his wife of ten years, Meghan, and their two young daughters, Kensington and Campbell.

ALL · IN · ONE

AWS Certified Cloud Practitioner

EXAM GUIDE

(Exam CLF-C01)

Daniel Carter

New York   Chicago   San Francisco
Athens   London   Madrid   Mexico City
Milan   New Delhi   Singapore   Sydney   Toronto

McGraw Hill books are available at special quantity discounts to use as premiums and sales promotions, or for use in corporate training programs. To contact a representative, please visit the Contact Us pages at www.mhprofessional.com.

AWS Certified Cloud Practitioner All-in-One Exam Guide (Exam CLF-C01)

1 2 3 4 5 6 7 8 9   LCR   25 24 23 22 20

Library of Congress Control Number: 2020949146

ISBN   978-1-260-47387-2
MHID   1-260-47387-2

Sponsoring Editor	Technical Editor	Production Supervisor
Lisa McClain	Taylor York	Lynn M. Messina
Editorial Supervisor	**Copy Editor**	**Composition**
Patty Mon	Lisa McCoy	KnowledgeWorks Global Ltd.
Project Manager	**Proofreader**	**Illustration**
Parag Mittal,	Vicki Wong	KnowledgeWorks Global Ltd.
KnowledgeWorks Global Ltd.	**Indexer**	**Art Director, Cover**
Acquisitions Coordinator	Ted Laux	Jeff Weeks
Emily Walters		

This book is dedicated to my children—Zachariah, Malachi, Alannah, and Ezra. I love you all so much and look forward to seeing how each of you four very unique souls will change the world for the better!

CONTENTS AT A GLANCE

CONTENTS

ACKNOWLEDGMENTS

This is my third book and my first foray into AWS. I first want to thank Matt Walker for connecting me to the opportunity with my first book and encouraging me to take it on. I hope that you find this book to be an informative and comprehensive aid in your own professional development and growth.

I owe a special thanks for my technical editor on this book, Taylor York, for always steering me in the right direction with AWS and keeping me focused on the right perspective when presenting AWS technologies and how to approach them.

I worked with David Henry for many years at the University of Maryland and gained much of my knowledge about middleware and systems architecture from him. I owe much of my philosophy and approach to facing IT challenges today to the things I learned working for and with him. There are so many others from my days at the University of Maryland from whom I learned so much. However, I want to specifically call out John Pfeifer, David Arnold, Spence Spencer, Kevin Hildebrand, Prasad Dharmasena, Fran LoPresti, Eric Sturdivant, Willie Brown, Sonja Kueppers, Ira Gold, and Brian Swartzfager.

From my time at the Centers for Medicare & Medicaid Services (CMS), I want to specifically thank Jon Booth and Ketan Patel for giving me the opportunity to move into a formal security position for the first time and trusting me to oversee incredibly public and visible systems. Also, thanks to Zabeen Chong for giving me the opportunity to join CMS and expand beyond my roots in the academic world. Finally, I could never leave out my dear friend Andy Trusz, who from my first day at CMS showed me the ropes of the workplace and became a very close personal friend. Sadly, he lost his battle with cancer the very day I left CMS for Hewlett Packard Enterprise. I will never forget his friendship and all he showed me!

With any project of this scale, one needs enormous support and understanding from bosses and coworkers. Ruth Pine was a terrific boss, giving me the time and freedom to work on my original books and was always very supportive, as well as giving me the opportunity at all times to work on new challenges and expand my areas of expertise, most notably with cloud and SIEM technologies. Thanks also to Brian Moore, Joe Fuhrman, Steve Larson, BJ Kerlavage, David Kohlway, Seref Konur, Jack Schatoff, and the already mentioned Matt Walker for being part of an amazing team at HPE/DXC/Perspecta and showing me so many different perspectives and new approaches to challenges! I also have to thank some colleagues from other companies I have worked closely with on projects over the years for all their support and encouragement—specifically, Anna Tant, Jason Ashbaugh, and Richie Frieman.

Three years ago, I was presented with the opportunity to get back to my roots in the academic world with a terrific job at Johns Hopkins University working with the Enterprise Authentication team on SSO and federated identity systems. With a large hospital, this was an ideal opportunity to combine my experience working in healthcare. I want to thank my director, Andy Baldwin, for this opportunity; my manager, Anthony Reid; and the amazing team I work with: Etan Weintraub, Stephen Molczyk, Kevin Buckley, Sam Bennett, John Clark, Brian Schisler, Michael Goldberg, and Dotun Adeoson. I would also like to thank Tyge Goodfellow, Eric Wunder, Steve Metheny, Phil Bearmen, and Dawn Hayes for expanding my security and IDM knowledge in many different directions!

Thank you to my parents, Richard and Susan, for all of your support and encouragement!

Last and most certainly not least, I want to thank my amazing wife, Robyn, for always being supportive with everything I have done professionally and personally. With four young kids at home, I would have never been able to even consider this project without her help and understanding—and for running interference with all our kids and pets!

INTRODUCTION

Over the last several years, the term *cloud* has become common in the modern lexicon of even lay persons with no connection to, training in, or expertise in the IT industry. It has become common in commercials targeting the public at large and is often used as a main selling point for various services. Even those who do not understand what cloud computing is or how it works have largely come to understand it as a positive feature for a product or service, feeling it means higher reliability, speed, and an overall more beneficial consumer experience. Many companies are flocking to cloud computing at a rapid pace due to its benefits and features.

With this enormous paradigm shift in the industry, the demand for skilled professionals who understand cloud computing has grown at a similarly rapid pace. This demand applies to professionals in all facets of computing, but the unique aspects and features of cloud computing make the need for skilled personnel paramount to any organization in order to properly design, provision, leverage, and protect their systems, applications, and data.

Cloud computing represents a paradigm shift in how IT experts look at leveraging resources and data and the various techniques, methodologies, and cost models available to them. Some of you approaching this certification are experienced security professionals and already hold other certifications. For others, this certification will be your first. Some of you have been working with cloud computing from its onset, while others are learning the basics of cloud for the first time. This certification guide aims to fulfill the requirements of anyone approaching this challenging exam, regardless of background or specific experience in IT.

This guide will give you the information you need to pass the AWS Certified Cloud Practitioner exam, but it will also expand your understanding and knowledge of cloud computing and security beyond just being able to answer specific exam questions. The structure of this *All-in-One* aligns closely with and provides complete coverage of the AWS exam objectives. You also get an appendix with a full-length practice exam. My hope is that you will find this guide to be a reference that serves you long past this specific exam.

Regardless of your background, experience, and certifications, I hope you find the world of cloud computing and its capabilities and challenges to be both enlightening and intellectually stimulating. Cloud represents a dynamic, exciting new direction in computing and one that is certain to be a major paradigm for the foreseeable future.

Objective Map

The objective map included in Appendix A has been constructed to help you cross-reference the official exam objectives from AWS with the relevant coverage in the book. Official exam objectives have been provided exactly as AWS has presented them with the corresponding chapter that covers that objective.

Online Practice Exams

This book includes access to online practice exams that feature the TotalTester Online exam test engine, which allows you to generate a complete practice exam or to generate quizzes by chapter or by exam domain. See Appendix C for more information and instructions on how to access the exam tool.

Becoming an AWS Certified Cloud Practitioner

In this chapter, you will learn about the following topics:
- Why the AWS CCP certification is valuable
- How to obtain the AWS CCP certification
- An introduction to the four AWS CCP domains

As cloud computing has exploded in use and popularity, so has the demand for employees that have a sound understanding of how it works and its key aspects. AWS has long been a leader in cloud and is the most synonymous platform with it. The AWS Certified Cloud Practitioner (CCP) was designed for individuals to show they have a broad understanding of AWS, its key services, and how to operate within its environment and tools.

Why Get Certified?

Obtaining a certification that is widely known and respected demonstrates to employers that you have a certain level of understanding and education about the material it encompasses. With cloud computing growing so rapidly, many jobs will look for employees with an understanding and familiarity with AWS, and the CCP is an excellent way to independently show that you have this. The AWS CCP will serve individuals that work in IT, but also those outside of IT that want to demonstrate that they understand AWS and can offer value to themselves, their employers, prospective clients, and others through this knowledge. The AWS CCP servers as a first AWS certification that can start you on your path to more advanced and specialized certifications offered on the AWS platform.

How to Get Certified

As a first certification for the AWS platform, the AWS CCP does not have required work-experience time as a prerequisite, though it is highly recommended that you have six months of experience working with AWS in some capacity. This can range from IT professionals to students, business professionals, project managers, marketing specialists, and even legal professionals. Candidates should also have a basic understanding of IT and IT services in order to relate these concepts to the AWS Cloud environment.

In order to successfully pass the AWS CCP exam, a candidate will be expected to demonstrate the following:

- Explain the value of AWS Cloud services
- Understand and be able to explain the AWS Shared Responsibility Model and how it would apply to their business or job
- Understand and be able to explain security best practices for AWS accounts and management consoles
- Understand how pricing, costs, and budgets are done within AWS, including the tools that AWS provides for monitoring and tracking them
- Be able to describe the core and popular AWS service offerings across the major areas of network, compute, storage, databases, and development
- Be able to recommend and justify which AWS core services would apply to real-world scenarios

The AWS CCP exam consists of 65 questions with a 90-minute exam time limit. The current cost of the exam is $100 USD.

The following information applies to the exam content:

- The exam consists of two types of questions:
  - Multiple choice: Each question has four possible answers, only one of which is correct.
  - Multiple response: Each question has five or more possible answers, two or more of which are correct.
- Unscored content
  - Some questions are included for trial or research purposes that are not scored as part of your examination.
  - You will not know which questions fall into this category.
- Any unanswered question is scored by the exam as incorrect.

 EXAM TIP If you are unsure which answer is correct, try to eliminate as many as you can and then make a best guess from the remaining. A blank answer is scored the same as an incorrect answer, so making your best guess is always the best approach!

Once you have completed the exam, you will be given your results based upon a scoring of 100 to 1,000. You need a score of 700 to pass.

You will also receive a report that breaks down your performance on each section of the exam, so you can see which areas you were strongest in and which need improvement. However, the overall exam is based on a pass/fail determination. You do not need to perform to a certain level in each section—only overall do you need to reach a passing score. The number of questions from each section will generally follow the weighted distribution of content for the exam, so you will get more questions from some sections and fewer than others to reflect this.

AWS CCP Domains

The AWS CCP is divided into four different domains. The distribution of those domains and their weight of the overall exam content are shown in the following table.

Domain	% of Exam
Domain 1: Cloud Concepts	26%
Domain 2: Security and Compliance	25%
Domain 3: Technology	33%
Domain 4: Billing and Pricing	16%
TOTAL	100%

Domain 1: Cloud Concepts

Domain 1 will introduce you to the AWS and the value it can bring to your organization. Before you attempt to sell your stakeholders on the value AWS can bring to your organization, you need to have a full understanding of what AWS is, the value it offers, how it is structured and designed, and how it differs from the traditional data center model. This chapter will give you a sound basis and show you how to get started with using AWS from the ground up by giving you an understanding of cloud concepts.

Domain 2: Security and Compliance

Domain 2 focuses on how security is a primary focus for AWS across all services and one of the most prominent benefits of using a cloud provider. AWS can implement extremely robust security through economies of scale that can far exceed what any organization could have the finances and experience to implement on their own. This domain will introduce you to the Shared Responsibility Model that cloud providers employ, as well as the key concepts used with cloud security. We will cover the specific implementations of these concepts by AWS and the resources available to users for security support.

Domain 3: Technology

Domain 3 covers the technical aspects of the AWS Cloud. This includes the tools and utilities to get users up and running in AWS, as well as code development. The core AWS services are highlighted, along with their key features and how they can improve the on-premises hosting and operating models that most companies already use. Many support options are available for AWS technical aspects, including support plans, documentation, and user forums.

Domain 4: Billing and Pricing

Domain 4 covers the many different pricing models that AWs offers across all of their services, focusing on the unifying fact that costs are only incurred for resources that are provisioned and only while they are being used. With the complexity of services and all the possible cost points, AWS provides management tools to estimate, plan, and track usage of both services and budgets to allow users to stay on top of their costs. This includes both the AWS Free Tier and paid services.

Chapter Review

This first chapter covered the value in obtaining the AWS CCP certification, as well as the steps required to earn it. We covered the details of the exam, the distribution of material on it, and the types of questions that are used. We also covered the requirements to pass the AWS CCP exam and how the scores are broken down. Lastly, we covered a brief introduction of each domain of the AWS CCP.

Cloud Concepts

In this chapter, you will learn the following Domain 1 topics:
- Define the AWS Cloud and its value proposition
- Identity aspects of AWS Cloud Economics
- List the different cloud architecture design principles

This chapter will introduce you to the AWS Cloud and what value it can bring to your organization and operations. Before you attempt to sell your stakeholders on the value AWS can bring to your organization, you need to have a full understanding of what AWS is, the value it offers, how it is structured and designed, and how it differs from the traditional data center model. This chapter will give you a sound basis and show you how to get started with using AWS from the ground up by giving you an understanding of cloud concepts.

What Is Cloud Computing?

The term "cloud" is heard almost everywhere in media and business today, from popular culture to corporate board rooms. Whether it is the old Microsoft commercials of a few years ago with the mantra of "take it to the cloud!" or the use of common applications, such as iCloud, OneDrive, or Gmail, the term has become ubiquitous in modern life. Most people you will ever run into, whether they are students or seasoned IT professionals, will be well inundated with the idea of the cloud, even if they have scant knowledge of what it actually is or does.

The National Institute of Standards and Technology (NIST) of the United States has published Special Publication (SP) 800-145, "The NIST Definition of Cloud Computing," which gives their official definition of the cloud:

> Cloud computing is a model for enabling ubiquitous, convenient, on-demand network access to a shared pool of configurable computer resources (e.g., networks, servers, storage, applications, and services) that can be rapidly provisioned and released with minimal management effort or service provider interaction. This cloud model is composed of five essential characteristics, three service models, and four deployment models.

Rather than the classic data center model with server hardware, network appliances, cabling, power units, and environmental controls, cloud computing is predicated on the concept of purchasing "services" to comprise various levels of automation and support based on the needs of the customer at any point in time. This is in contrast to the classical data center model, which requires a customer to purchase and configure systems for their maximum capacity at all times, regardless of need, due to business cycles and changing demands.

Cloud Computing Concepts

Before we dive into more thorough discussions of cloud concepts and capabilities, it is important to lay a strong foundation of cloud computing definitions first via a general overview of the technologies involved.

Cloud Computing Definitions

The following list presents some introductory definitions for this chapter, based on ISO/IEC 17788, "Cloud Computing—Overview and Vocabulary." Many more definitions will be given later (see also the glossary in this book).

- **Cloud application** An application that does not reside or run on a user's device, but rather is accessible via a network.
- **Cloud application portability** The ability to migrate a cloud application from one cloud provider to another.
- **Cloud computing** A network-accessible platform that delivers services from a large and scalable pool of systems, rather than dedicated physical hardware and more static configurations.
- **Cloud data portability** The ability to move data between cloud providers.
- **Cloud deployment model** How cloud computing is delivered through a set of particular configurations and features of virtual resources. The cloud deployment models are public, private, hybrid, and community.
- **Data portability** The ability to move data from one system to another without having to re-enter it.
- **Infrastructure as a Service (IaaS)** A cloud service category where infrastructure-level services are provided by a cloud service provider.
- **Measured service** Cloud services are delivered and billed for in a metered way.
- **Multitenancy** Having multiple customers and applications running within the same environment but in a way that they are isolated from each other and not visible to each other but share the same resources.
- **On-demand self-service** A cloud customer can provision services in an automatic manner, when needed, with minimal involvement from the cloud provider.
- **Platform as a Service (PaaS)** A cloud service category where platform services are provided to the cloud customer, and the cloud provider is responsible for the system up to the level of the actual application.

- **Resource pooling**   The aggregation of resources allocated to cloud customers by the cloud provider.
- **Reversibility**   The ability of a cloud customer to remove all data and applications from a cloud provider and completely remove all data from their environment.
- **Software as a Service (SaaS)**   Cloud service category in which a full application is provided to the cloud customer, and the cloud provider maintains responsibility for the entire infrastructure, platform, and application.
- **Tenant**   One or more cloud customers sharing access to a pool of resources.

Cloud Computing Roles

These definitions represent the basic and most important roles within a cloud system and the relationships between them, based on ISO/IEC 17788. You will see many of these used throughout any materials relating to cloud computing.

- **Cloud auditor**   An auditor that is specifically responsible for conducting audits of cloud systems and cloud applications.
- **Cloud service broker**   A partner that servers as an intermediary between a cloud service customer and cloud service provider.
- **Cloud service customer**   One that holds a business relationship for services with a cloud service provider.
- **Cloud service partner**   One that holds a relationship with either a cloud service provider or a cloud service customer to assist with cloud services and their delivery.
- **Cloud service provider**   One that offers cloud services to cloud service customers.
- **Cloud service user**   One that interacts with and consumes services offered by a cloud services customer.

Key Cloud Computing Characteristics

Cloud computing has six essential characteristics. In order for an implementation to be considered a cloud in a true sense, each of these six characteristics must be present and operational:

- On-demand self-service
- Broad network access
- Resource pooling
- Rapid elasticity
- Metered service
- Multitenancy

Each of these characteristics is discussed in more detail in the following sections.

On-Demand Self-Service

Cloud services can be requested, provisioned, and put into use by the customer through automated means without the need to interact with a person. This is typically offered by the cloud provider through a web portal but can also be provided in some cases through web application programming interface (API) calls or other programmatic means. As services are expanded or contracted, billing is adjusted through automatic means.

In the sense of billing, this does not just apply to large companies or firms that have contractual agreements with cloud providers for services and open lines of credit or financing agreements. Even small businesses and individuals can take advantage of the same services through such simple arrangements as having a credit card on file and an awareness of the cloud provider's terms and charges, and many systems will tell the user at the time of the request what the additional and immediate costs will be.

Self-service comprises an integral component of the "pay-as-you-go" nature of cloud computing and the convergence of computing resources as a utility service.

Broad Network Access

All cloud services and components are accessible over the network and accessible in most cases through many different vectors. This ability for heterogeneous access through a variety of clients is a hallmark of cloud computing, where services are provided while staying agnostic to the access methods of the consumers. In the case of cloud computing, services can be accessed typically from either web browsers or thick or thin clients, regardless of whether the consumer is using a mobile device, laptop, or desktop and either from a corporate network or from a personal device on an open network.

The cloud revolution in computing has occurred concurrently with the mobile computing revolution, making the importance of being agnostic concerning the means of access a top priority. Because many companies have begun allowing bring-your-own-device (BYOD) access to their corporate IT systems, it is imperative that any environments they operate within be able to support a wide variety of platforms and software clients.

 CAUTION BYOD can be a major headache for IT security professionals. It is often seen by management as a cost-cutting method or a way to appease employees regarding their personal access, but it adds a host of additional concerns to any network or application regarding secure access methods. In a cloud environment, BYOD can potentially be less of an issue, depending on the type of cloud model employed, but it always must be safely monitored. Cloud storage also alleviates the need for users to store their data on their devices and instead access it via the network, thus increasing security by removing data storage physically from the device. AWS also offers high-performance cloud desktops that can be accessed from other devices or low-performance PCs, which can help an organization with BYOD.

Resource Pooling

One of the most important concepts in cloud computing is resource pooling, or multitenancy. In a cloud environment, regardless of the type of cloud offering, you always will have a mix of applications and systems that coexist within the same set of physical and virtual resources. As cloud customers add to and expand their usage within the cloud, the new resources are dynamically allocated within the cloud, and the customer has no control over (and, really, no need to know) where the actual services are deployed. This aspect of the cloud can apply to any type of service deployed within the environment, including processing, memory, network utilization, and devices, as well as storage. At the time of provisioning, services can and will be automatically deployed throughout the cloud infrastructure, and mechanisms are in place for locality and other requirements based on the particular needs of the customer and any regulatory or legal requirements that they be physically housed in a particular country or data center. However, these will have been configured within the provisioning system via contract requirements before they are actually requested by the customer, and then they are provisioned within those rules by the system without the customer needing to specify them at that time.

Many corporations have computing needs that are cyclical in nature. With resource pooling and a large sample of different systems that are utilized within the same cloud infrastructure, companies can have the resources they need on their own cycles without having to build out systems to handle the maximum projected load, which means these resources won't sit unused and idle at other nonpeak times. Significant cost savings can be realized for all customers of the cloud through resource pooling and the economies of scale that it affords.

TIP From my own experience working for an academic institution and in healthcare, the cyclical nature of computing needs is a huge benefit of cloud computing. In both environments, you have defined periods of the year with greatly increased loads and slow periods for most of the rest of the year. Having resources pooled and available when needed is a huge benefit.

Rapid Elasticity

With cloud computing being decoupled from hardware and with the programmatic provisioning capabilities, services can be rapidly expanded at any time additional resources are needed. This capability can be provided through the web portal or initiated on behalf of the customer, either in response to an expected or projected increase in the demand of services or during such an increase in demand; the decision to change scale is balanced against the funding and capabilities of the customer. If the applications and systems are built in a way where they can be supported, elasticity can be automatically implemented such that the cloud provider, through programmatic means and based on predetermined metrics, can automatically scale the system by adding resources and can bill the customer accordingly.

In a classic data center model, a customer needs to have ready and configured enough computing resources at all times to handle any potential and projected load on their systems. Along with what was previously mentioned under "Resource Pooling," many companies that have cyclical and defined periods of heavy load can run leaner systems during off-peak times and then scale up, either manually or automatically, as the need arises. A prime example of this would be applications that handle healthcare enrollment or university class registrations. In both cases, the systems have very heavy peak use periods and largely sit idle the remainder of the year.

Metered Service

Depending on the type of service and cloud implementation, resources are metered and logged for billing and utilization reporting. This metering can be done in a variety of ways and using different aspects of the system, or even multiple methods. This can include storage, network, memory, processing, the number of nodes or virtual machines, and the number of users. Within the terms of the contract and agreements, these metrics can be used for a variety of uses, such as monitoring and reporting, placing limitations on resource utilization, and setting thresholds for automatic elasticity. These metrics also will be used to some degree in determining the provider's adherence to the requirements set forth in the service level agreement (SLA).

Many large companies as a typical practice use internal billing of individual systems based on the usage of their data centers and resources. This is especially true with companies that contract IT services to other companies or government agencies. In a classic data center model with physical hardware, this was much more difficult to achieve in a meaningful way. With the metering and reporting metrics that cloud providers are able to offer, this becomes much more simplistic for companies and offers a significantly greater degree of flexibility, with granularity of systems and expansion.

Multitenancy

A traditional data center model typically has physical separation between different customers. In most cases, this is done through cages and completely separate network gear. However, a cloud environment can have many different customers running resources and applications within the same physical hardware devices and rely on virtual and logical segregation within the hosting model instead. Many customers will also use multiple tenants within a cloud environment to segregate different types of environments or services. This can be done to either isolate different offices or applications but also is commonly used for test or development environments.

Building-Block Technologies

Regardless of the service category or deployment model used for a cloud implementation, the core components and building blocks are the same. Any cloud implementation at a fundamental level is composed of processor or CPU, memory/RAM, networking, and storage solutions. Depending on the cloud service category, the cloud customer will have varying degrees of control over or responsibility for those building blocks. The next section introduces the three main cloud service categories and goes into detail about what the cloud customer has access to or responsibility for.

Virtualization

Virtualization is what makes cloud computing, and the key aspects of it, a reality. In a traditional data center model with servers, each system is a physical piece of equipment with static resources and abilities, based upon the components used to construct it. With traditional servers, if a particular system needs more memory, storage, or CPU, the only option an administrator had was to physically buy new components and add them to the system. On top of that, it would only work if the system were able to expand to meet the new demands; otherwise, a company would have to buy an entirely new system with greater capabilities.

With cloud computing, everything is in a shared environment with pooled resources. If a system needs to increase capacity for storage, memory, or CPU, no one has to add hardware components. When a request is made by a cloud customer through an automated web portal or other similar system, resources are automatically allocated to a virtual machine from the large pool of resources. This capability fully enables a company to always have the resources they need, as well as responding to cyclical demands and saving money during slower periods where resources can be deallocated until needed again.

Underlying the infrastructure in a cloud environment does ultimately have physical assets and resources that have limitations. However, this is joined together into a seamless virtual environment where resources are shared collectively. If particular host systems are running low on resources, virtual machines can automatically and dynamically be moved around without any intervention of administrators and completely transparent to users of the systems. This also allows for additional hosts to be added and the system rebalanced across the infrastructure in a seamless manner.

 EXAM TIP   Make sure to always look at computing within a cloud environment through the eyes of virtualization. While there are many similarities with systems in a cloud environment versus a traditional data center model, the underlying aspects of virtualization always prevail when pertaining to cloud computing, and the differences with virtualization are central to any considerations of the cloud.

Cloud Service Categories

Although many different terms are used for the specific types of cloud service models and offerings, three main models are universally accepted:

- Infrastructure as a Service (IaaS)
- Platform as a Service (PaaS)
- Software as a Service (SaaS)

Infrastructure as a Service

IaaS is the most basic cloud service and the one where the most customization and control are available for the customer. Within the AWS environment, IaaS products include Amazon Elastic Compute Cloud (EC2), Elastic Block Store (EBS), and Elastic Load Balancing.

The following is from the NIST SP 800-145 definition for IaaS:

> The capability provided to the consumer is to provision processing, storage, networks, and other fundamental computing resources where the consumer is able to deploy and run arbitrary software, which can include operating systems and applications. The consumer does not manage or control the underlying cloud infrastructure but has control over operating systems, storage, and deployed applications; and possibly limited control of selected networking components (e.g., host firewalls).

Key Features and Benefits of IaaS

The following are the key features and benefits of IaaS. Some key features overlap with other cloud service models, but others are unique to IaaS.

- **Scalability**   Within an IaaS framework, the system can be rapidly provisioned and expanded as needed, either for predictable events or in response to unexpected demand.

- **Cost of ownership of physical hardware**   Within IaaS, the customer does not need to procure any hardware either for the initial launch and implementation or for future expansion.

- **High availability**   The cloud infrastructure, by definition, meets high availability and redundancy requirements, which would result in additional costs for a customer to meet within their own data center.

- **Physical and logical security requirements**   Because you're in a cloud environment and don't have your own data centers, the cloud provider assumes the cost and oversight of the physical security of its data centers. Data is also protected by layers of logical network security and user access security (IAM).

- **Location and access independence**   The cloud-based infrastructure has no dependence on the physical location of the customer or users of the system, as well as no dependence on specific network locations or applications or clients to access the system. The only dependency is on the security requirements of the cloud itself and the applications settings used.

- **Metered usage**   The customer only pays for the resources they are using and only during the durations of use. There is no need to have large data centers with idle resources for large chunks of time just to cover heavy-load periods.

- **Potential for "green" data centers**   Many customers and companies are interested in having more environmentally friendly data centers that are high efficiency in terms of both power consumption and cooling. Within cloud environments, many providers have implemented "green" data centers that are more cost-effective with the economies of scale that would prohibit many customers from having their own. Although this is not a requirement for a cloud provider, many major providers do market this as a feature, which is of interest to many customers.

- **Choice of hardware**   AWS offers traditional Intel-based processors, but also offers AMD, GPU, and ARM processor options. Each option has its own scaling and configuration options.

Platform as a Service

PaaS allows a customer to fully focus on their core business functions from the software and application levels, either in development or production environments, without having to worry about the resources at the typical data center operations level. Within the AWS environment, PaaS offerings include Elastic Beanstalk.

The following is from the NIST SP 800-145 definition of PaaS:

> The capability provided to the customer is to deploy onto the cloud infrastructure consumer-created or acquired applications created using programming languages, libraries, services, and tools supported by the provider. The customer does not manage or control the underlying cloud infrastructure including network, servers, operating systems, or storage, but has control over the deployed applications and possibly configuration settings for the application-hosting environment.

Key Features and Benefits of PaaS

The following are the key features of the PaaS cloud service model. Although there is some overlap with IaaS and SaaS, each model has its own unique set of features and details.

- **Auto-scaling**   As resources are needed (or not needed), the system can automatically adjust the sizing of the environment to meet demand without interaction from the customer. This is especially important for those systems whose load is cyclical in nature, and it allows an organization to only configure and use what is actually needed so as to minimize idle resources.

- **Multiple host environments**   With the cloud provider responsible for the actual platform, the customer has a wide choice of operating systems and environments. This feature allows software and application developers to test or migrate their systems between different environments to determine the most suitable and efficient platform for their applications to be hosted under without having to spend time configuring and building new systems on physical servers. Because the customer only pays for the resources they are using in the cloud, different platforms can be built and tested without a long-term or expensive commitment by the customer. This also allows a customer evaluating different applications to be more open to underlying operating system requirements.

- **Choice of environments**   Most organizations have a set of standards for what their operations teams will support and offer as far as operating systems and platforms are concerned. This limits the options for application environments and operating system platforms that a customer can consider, both for homegrown and commercial products. The choice of environments not only extends to actual operating systems, but it also allows enormous flexibility as to specific versions and flavors of operating systems, contingent on what the cloud provider offers and supports.

- **Flexibility**   In a traditional data center setting, application developers are constrained by the offerings of the data center and are locked into proprietary systems that make relocation or expansion difficult and expensive. With those layers abstracted in a PaaS model, the developers have enormous flexibility to move between providers and platforms with ease. With many software applications and environments now open-source or built by commercial companies to run on a variety of platforms, PaaS offers development teams enormous ease in testing and moving between platforms or even cloud providers.

- **Ease of upgrades**   With the underlying operating systems and platforms being offered by the cloud provider, upgrades and changes are simpler and more efficient than in a traditional data center model, where system administrators need to perform actual upgrades on physical servers, which also means downtime and loss of productivity during upgrades.

- **Cost-effective**   Like with other cloud categories, PaaS offers significant cost savings for development teams because only systems that are actively and currently used incur costs. Additional resources can be added or scaled back as needed during development cycles in a quick and efficient manner.

- **Ease of access**   With cloud services being accessible from the Internet and regardless of access clients, development teams can easily collaborate across national and international boundaries without needing to obtain accounts or access to propriety corporate data centers. The location and access methods of development teams become irrelevant from a technological perspective, but the Certified Cloud Security Professional needs to be cognizant of any potential contractual or regulatory requirements. For example, with many government contracts, there may be requirements that development teams or hosting of systems and data be constrained within certain geographic or political borders.

- **Licensing**   In a PaaS environment, the cloud provider is responsible for handling proper licensing of operating systems and platforms, which would normally be incumbent on an organization to ensure compliance. Within a PaaS cloud model, those costs are assumed as part of the metered costs for services and incumbent on the cloud provider to track and coordinate with the vendors.

Software as a Service

SaaS is a fully functioning software application for a customer to use in a turnkey operation, where all the underlying responsibilities and operations for maintaining systems, patches, and operations are abstracted from the customer and are the responsibility of the cloud services provider. The following is from the NIST SP 800-145 definition of SaaS:

> The capability provided to the customer is to use the provider's applications running on a cloud infrastructure. The applications are accessible from various client devices through either a thin client interface, such as a web browser (e.g., web-based email), or a program interface. The consumer does not manage or control the underlying cloud infrastructure including network, servers, operating systems, storage, or even individual application capabilities, with the possible exception of limited user-specific application settings.

SaaS offerings are the most commonly known to consumers, as they are some of the most popular services and products used on mobile devices, such as iCloud, Dropbox, Gmail, etc.

Key Features and Benefits of SaaS

The following are the key features and benefits of the SaaS cloud service model. Some are similar to those of IaaS and PaaS, but due to the nature of SaaS being a fully built software platform, certain aspects are unique to SaaS.

- **Support costs and efforts**   In the SaaS service category, the cloud services are solely the responsibility of the cloud provider. Because the customer only licenses access to the software platform and capabilities, the entire underlying system, from network to storage and operating systems, as well as the software and application platforms themselves, is entirely removed from the responsibility of the consumer. Only the availability of the software application is important to the customer, and any responsibility for upgrades, patching, high availability, and operations solely reside with the cloud provider. This enables the customer to focus solely on productivity and business operations instead of IT operations.

- **Reduced overall costs**   The customer in a SaaS environment is only licensing use of the software. The customer does not need to have systems administrators or security staff on hand, nor do they need to purchase hardware and software, plan for redundancy and disaster recovery, perform security audits on infrastructure, or deal with utility and environmental costs. Apart from licensing access for appropriate resources, features, and user counts from the cloud provider, the only cost concern for the customer is training in the use of the application platform and the device or computer access that their employees or users need to use the system.

- **Licensing**   Similar to PaaS, within a SaaS model, the licensing costs are the responsibility of the cloud provider. Whereas PaaS offers the licensing of the operating system and platforms to the cloud provider, SaaS takes it a step further with the software and everything included, leaving the customer to just "lease" licenses as they consume resources within the provided application. This removes both the bookkeeping and individual costs of licenses from the customer's perspective and instead rolls everything into the single cost of utilization of the actual software platform. This model allows the cloud provider, based on the scale of their implementations, to also negotiate far more beneficial bulk licensing savings than a single company or user would ever be able to do on their own and thus drive lower total costs to their customers as well.

- **Ease of use and administration**   With SaaS implementations being a fully featured software installation and product, the cost and efforts of administration are substantially lowered compared to a PaaS or IaaS model. The customer only bears responsibility for configuring user access and access controls within the system, as well as minimal configurations. The configurations typically allowed within a SaaS system are usually very restricted and may only allow slight tweaks to the user experience, such as default settings or possibly some degree of branding; otherwise, all overhead and operations are held by the cloud provider exclusively.

- **Standardization**   Because SaaS is a fully featured software application, all users will, by definition, be running the exact same version of the software at all times. A major challenge that many development and implementation teams face relates to patching and versioning, as well as configuration baselines and requirements. Within a SaaS model, because this is all handled by the cloud provider, it is achieved automatically.

 EXAM TIP   The vast majority of services offered by AWS are IaaS or PaaS implementations. Make sure you fully understand the SaaS model as well, however, as it will help you understand how many very popular consumer services are built and operate, as well as how they may interact with other types of implementations.

Cloud Deployment Models

There are four main types of cloud deployment and hosting models in common use, each of which can host any of the three main cloud service models.

Public Cloud

A public cloud is just what it sounds like. It is a model that provides cloud services to the general public or any company or organization at large without restriction beyond finances and planning. The following is the NIST SP 800-145 definition:

> The cloud infrastructure is provisioned for open use by the general public. It may be owned, managed, and operated by a business, academic, or government organization, or some combination of them. It exists on the premises of the cloud provider.

Key Benefits and Features of the Public Cloud Model

The following are key and unique benefits and features of the public cloud model:

- **Setup**   Setup is very easy and inexpensive for the customer. All aspects of infrastructure, including hardware, network, licensing, bandwidth, and operational costs, are controlled and assumed by the provider.
- **Scalability**   Even though scalability is a common feature of all cloud implementations, most public clouds are offered from very large corporations that have very broad and extensive resources and infrastructures. This allows even large implementations the freedom to scale as needed and as budgets allow, without worry of hitting capacity or interfering with other hosted implementations on the same cloud.
- **Right-sizing resources**   Customers only pay for what they use and need at any given point in time. Their sole investment is scoped to their exact needs and can be completely fluid and agile over time based on either expected demand or unplanned demand at any given point in time.

Private Cloud

A private cloud differs from a public cloud in that it is run by and restricted to the organization that it serves. A private cloud model may also be opened up to other entities, expanding outward for developers, employees, contractors, and subcontractors, as well as potential collaborators and other firms that may offer complementary services or subcomponents. The following is the NIST SP 800-145 definition:

> The cloud infrastructure is provisioned for exclusive use by a single organization comprising multiple consumers (e.g., business units). It may be owned, managed, and operated by the organization, a third party, or some combination of them, and it may exist on or off premises.

Key Benefits and Features of the Private Cloud Model

The following are key benefits and features of the private cloud model and how it differs from a public cloud:

- **Ownership retention** Because the organization that utilizes the cloud also owns and operates it and controls who has access to it, that organization retains full control over it. This includes control of the underlying hardware and software infrastructures, as well as control throughout the cloud in regard to data policies, access polices, encryption methods, versioning, change control, and governance as a whole. For any organization that has strict policies or regulatory controls and requirements, this model would facilitate easier compliance and verification for auditing purposes versus the more limited controls and views offered via a public cloud. In cases where contracts or regulations stipulate locality and limitations as to where data and systems may reside and operate, a private cloud ensures compliance with requirements beyond just the contractual controls that a public cloud might offer, which also would require extensive reporting and auditing to validate compliance.

- **Control over systems** With a private cloud, the operations and system parameters of the cloud are solely at the discretion of the controlling organization. Whereas in a public cloud model an organization would be limited to the specific offerings for software and operating system versions, as well as patch and upgrade cycles, a private cloud allows the organization to determine what versions and timelines are offered without the need for contractual negotiations or potentially increased costs if specific versions need to be retained and supported beyond the time horizon that a public cloud is willing to offer.

- **Proprietary data and software control** Whereas a public cloud requires extensive software and contractual requirements to ensure the segregation and security of hosted systems, a private cloud offers absolute assurance that no other hosted environments can somehow gain access or insight into another hosted environment.

Community Cloud

A community cloud is a collaboration between similar organizations that combine resources to offer a private cloud. It is comparable to a private cloud with the exception of multiple ownership and/or control versus singular ownership of a private cloud. The following is the NIST SP 800-145 definition:

> The cloud infrastructure is provisioned for exclusive use by a specific community of consumers from organizations that have shared concerns (e.g., mission, security requirements, policy, and compliance considerations). It may be owned, managed, and operated by one or more of the organizations in the community, a third party, or some combination of them, and may exist on or off premises.

Hybrid Cloud

As the name implies, a hybrid cloud combines the use of both private and public cloud models to fully meet an organization's needs. The following is the NIST SP 800-145 definition:

> The cloud infrastructure is a composition of two or more distinct cloud infrastructures (private, community, or public) that remain unique entities, but are bound together by standardized or proprietary technology that enables data and application portability (e.g., cloud busting for load balancing between clouds).

Key Benefits and Features of the Hybrid Cloud Model

Building upon key features and benefits of the public and private cloud models, these are the key features of the hybrid model:

- **Split systems for optimization**   With a hybrid model, a customer has the opportunity and benefit of splitting out their operations between public and private clouds for optimal scaling and cost-effectiveness. If desired by the organization, some parts of systems can be maintained internally while leveraging the expansive offerings of public clouds for other systems. This can be done for cost reasons, security concerns, regulatory requirements, or to leverage toolsets and offerings that a public cloud may provide that their private cloud does not.

- **Flexibility in data processing**   Large volumes of data, such as terabytes of video data, can be processed locally, before uploading to the cloud, to save both network and processing resources.

- **Retain critical systems internally**   When a company has the option to leverage a public cloud and its services, critical data systems can be maintained internally with private data controls and access controls.

- **Disaster recovery**   An organization can leverage a hybrid cloud as a way to maintain systems within its own private cloud but utilize and have at its disposal the resources and options of a public cloud for disaster recovery and redundancy purposes. This would allow an organization to utilize its own private resources but have the ability to migrate systems to a public cloud when needed, without having to incur the costs of a failover site that sits idle except when an emergency arises. Because public cloud systems are only used in the event of a disaster, no costs would be incurred by the organization until such an event occurs. Also, with the organization building and maintaining its own images on its private cloud, these same images could be loaded into the provisioning system of a public cloud and be ready to use if and when required.

- **Scalability**   Along the same lines as disaster recovery usage, an organization can have at the ready a contract with a public cloud provider to handle periods of burst traffic, either forecasted or in reaction to unexpected demand. In this scenario, an organization can keep its systems internal with its private cloud but have the option to scale out to a public cloud on short notice, only incurring costs should the need arise.

EXAM TIP   While the nature of AWS and the way most people use and understand it is as a public cloud, make sure you understand how a hybrid cloud is used as well. Many companies will utilize hybrid cloud implementations for disaster recovery and business continuity planning but also to maintain flexibility for their operations and systems.

Cost-Benefit Analysis

This chapter has provided a broad overview of cloud computing and the various forms it can take. Any organization considering a move to a cloud environment should undertake a rigorous cost-benefit analysis to determine whether it is appropriate for their specific systems or applications, weighed against what a cloud can and cannot provide. In the following sections, we discuss several factors that figure prominently into any cost-benefit analysis.

Resource Pooling and Cyclical Demands

As previously mentioned, many organizations have a cyclical nature to their system demands to some extent or another. With a traditional data center, an organization has to maintain sufficient resources to handle their highest load peaks, which demands much larger up-front hardware and ongoing support costs. A move to a cloud environment would in this case be a benefit to a company in that they would only incur costs as needed, and the initial up-front costs would be far lower without having to build up a massive infrastructure from the outset. However, if a company has steady load throughout the year and is not susceptible to large bursts or cycles, then a move to a cloud environment may not yield the same level of benefits.

Data Center Costs vs. Operational Expense Costs

A typical data center setup for an organization carries expenses for facilities, utilities, systems staff, networking, storage, and all the components needed to run an operation from the ground up. In a cloud environment, with those components being largely or wholly the responsibility of the cloud provider, the focus is then shifted to management and oversight, as well as requirements for building and auditing. While the higher costs for data centers will be mitigated by a cloud, the customer will spend a far larger amount on operations and oversight in a cloud environment. It is important for any organization thinking about moving to a cloud environment to fully assess the staff and talents they already have and whether they can adapt to the new demands and changing roles in a cloud environment and whether they are willing and able to make those changes, either through training or staff changes.

Focus Change

Moving to a cloud environment brings a large degree of change in focus to an organization. Many organizations are structured in a manner that contains both operations and development staff. With a move to a cloud, the operations side will fundamentally change from running systems to overseeing them, as discussed previously. An organization will need to evaluate whether they are ready and able to make such a focus shift, as much of their upper management, policies, and organizational structure may well be built around functional focuses. A rush to a cloud environment could disrupt productivity; cause internal fighting; or even result in a significant loss of staff, talent, and corporate knowledge.

However, a move to a cloud carries enormous benefits from a change in culture as well. Developers can very easily take on new projects and try out new innovations with the ability to rapidly allocate resources, along with the broad range of options they have within a cloud environment. This can keep staff very motivated and excited about what they get to work on and the ability to quickly start projects without the traditional wait times and costs for hardware procurement and configuration.

NOTE The change in focus of an organization bridges all aspects and divisions within it. Whether you are from a technical background or not, always keep in mind this different focus and how you can apply it to your area of expertise and efforts.

Ownership and Control

When an organization owns their data centers and all the hardware, they get to set all the rules and have full control over everything. In a move to a cloud environment, the organization gives up direct control over operational procedures, system management, and maintenance, as well as upgrade plans and environment changes. While an organization can put in place strong contracts and SLA requirements, they still will not have the degree of flexibility and control that they would have in a proprietary data center. The organization will have to gauge the temperament and expectations of their management to determine whether this change is something that will be manageable over time or will cause bigger issues and tension.

However, major cloud providers such as AWS have enabled a heightened sense of ownership with the flexibility they offer for configurations and the broad range of options for resources. As compared to rented space in a traditional data center, AWS offers greater control than the limitations of renting rack space would typically offer. Coupled with the layers of network security through access control lists (ACLs) and security groups, along with robust Identity and Access Management (IAM), a move to the cloud can often bring an increased sense of ownership.

Cost Structure

Costs are very predictable in a traditional data center. An organization can appropriate funds for capital expenditures for hardware and infrastructure and then allocate appropriate staffing and resources to maintain the hardware and infrastructure over time. In a cloud environment with metered pricing, costs are realized as resources are added and changed over time. This can cause an unpredictable schedule of costs that may or may not work for a company and the way it handles finances internally. This is an aspect that will have to be carefully evaluated and understood by management. Different billing structures are available, or a middle contractor can be used to provide services that are priced on a longer-term basis, but that will vary greatly based on the needs and expectations of the organization.

Universal Cloud Concepts

Several aspects of cloud computing are universal, regardless of the particular service category or deployment model.

Interoperability

Interoperability is the ease with which one can move or reuse components of an application or service. The underlying platform, operating system, location, API structure, or cloud provider should not be an impediment to moving services easily and efficiently to an alternative solution. An organization that has a high degree of interoperability with its systems is not bound to one cloud provider and can easily move to another if the level of service or price is not suitable. This keeps pressure on cloud providers to offer a high level of services and to be competitive with pricing or risk losing customers to other cloud providers at any time. With services only incurring costs as they are used, it is even easier to change providers with a high degree of interoperability because long-term contracts are not set. Further, an organization also maintains flexibility to move between different cloud hosting models, such as moving from public to private clouds and vice versa, as its internal needs or requirements change over time. With an interoperability mandate, an organization can seamlessly move between cloud providers, underlying technologies, and hosting environments, or it can split components apart and host them in different environments without affecting the flow of data or services.

Elasticity and Scalability

Elasticity and scalability are similar concepts in terms of the changing of resources allocated to a system or application to meet current demands. The difference between the two concepts relates to the manner in which the level of resources is altered. With scalability, the allocated resources are changed statistically to meet anticipated demands or new deployments in services. Elasticity adds the ability for the dynamic modification of resources to meet demands as they evolve. With elasticity, a customer can set thresholds for when a cloud environment will automatically add or remove resources for unanticipated demands. Along with the allocation of resources comes the fluid changing of billing for a cloud customer. Careful attention must be given by a cloud customer to prevent the possible incurrence of large billing increases if unanticipated demands in increases occur, whether they materialize from legitimate customer usage or from attack attempts by malicious actors. With scalability, costs can be more easily managed, as resource allocations are only changed as they are made by an administrator—they are not automatically made by the system.

 EXAM TIP Elasticity and scalability are the two most important concepts from this section. Make sure you fully understand the differences between them and how they are used. An easy way to think about the two concepts is that a system is scalable if additional resources can be added with possible downtimes or restarts, but it is elastic if resources can be added seamlessly without needing downtime or restarts.

Performance, Availability, and Resiliency

The concepts of performance, availability, and resiliency should be considered de facto aspects of any cloud environment due to the nature of cloud infrastructures and models. Given the size and scale of most cloud implementations, performance should always be second nature to a cloud unless it is incorrectly planned or managed. Resiliency and high availability are also hallmarks of a cloud environment. If any of these areas fall short, customers will not stay long with a cloud provider and will quickly move to other providers. With proper provisioning and scaling by the cloud provider, performance should always be a top concern and focus. In a virtualized environment, it is easy for a cloud provider with proper management to move virtual machines and services around within its environment to maintain performance and even load. This capability is also what allows a cloud provider to maintain high availability and resiliency within its environment. As with many other key aspects of cloud computing, SLAs will determine and test the desired performance, availability, and resiliency of the cloud services.

 EXAM TIP The easiest way to remember the difference between availability and resiliency is the extent to which a system is affected by outages. Availability pertains to the overall status if a system is up or down, whereas resiliency pertains to the ability of a system to continue to function when some aspect or portions of it experience an outage. Resiliency can relate to either overall levels of resources, such as a loss of a percentage of virtual machines (VMs), or it can pertain to portions such as APIs or storage becoming unavailable.

Portability

Portability is the key feature that allows systems to easily and seamlessly move between different cloud providers. An organization that has its systems optimized for portability opens up enormous flexibility to move between different providers and hosting models and can be leveraged in a variety of ways. From a cost perspective, portability allows an organization to continually shop for cloud hosting services. Although cost can be a dominant driving factor, an organization may change providers for improved customer service, better feature sets and offerings, or SLA compliance issues. Apart from reasons to shop around for a cloud provider, portability also enables an organization to span their systems across multiple cloud hosting arrangements. This can be for disaster recovery reasons, locality diversity, or high availability, for example.

Service Level Agreements

Whereas a contract will spell out the general terms and costs for services, the SLA is where the real meat of the business relationship and concrete requirements come into play. The SLA spells out in clear terms the minimum requirements for uptime, availability, processes, customer service and support, security controls and requirements, auditing and reporting, and potentially many other areas that will define the business relationship and the success of it. Failure to meet the SLA requirements will give the customer either financial benefits or credits or form the basis for contract termination if acceptable performance cannot be rectified on behalf of the cloud provider.

Regulatory Requirements

Regulatory requirements are those imposed upon a business and its operations either by law, regulation, policy, or standards and guidelines. These requirements are specific to the locality in which the company or application is based or specific to the nature of the data and transactions conducted. These requirements can carry financial, legal, or even criminal penalties for failure to comply, either willfully or accidently. Sanctions and penalties can apply to the company itself or even in some cases the individuals working for the company and on its behalf, depending on the locality and the nature of the violation. Specific industries often have their own regulations and laws governing them above and beyond general regulations, such as the Health Insurance Portability and Accountability Act (HIPAA) in the healthcare sector, the Federal Information Security Management Act (FISMA) for U.S. federal agencies and contractors, and the Payment Card Industry Data Security Standard (PCI DSS) for the financial/retail sectors. These are just a few examples of specific regulations that go beyond general regulations that apply to all businesses. The Certified Cloud Security Professional needs to be aware of any and all regulations in which his or her systems and applications are required to comply; in most cases, failure to understand the requirements or ignorance of the requirements will not shield a company from investigations or penalties, or from potential damage to its reputation.

Security

Security is, of course, always a paramount concern for any system or application. Within a cloud environment, there can be a lot of management and stakeholder unease with using a newer technology, and many will be uncomfortable with the idea of having corporate and sensitive data not under direct control of internal IT staff and hardware housed in proprietary data centers. Depending on company policy and any regulatory or contractual requirements, different applications and systems will have their own specific security requirements and controls. Within a cloud environment, this becomes of particular interest because many customers are tenants within the same framework, and the cloud provider needs to ensure each customer that their controls are being met, and done so in a way that the cloud provider can support, with varying requirements. Another challenge exists with large cloud environments that likely have very strong security controls but will not publicly document what these controls are so as not to expose themselves to attacks. This is often mitigated within contract negotiations through non-disclosure agreements and privacy requirements, although this is still not the same level of understanding and information as an organization would have with its own internal and proprietary data centers.

The main way a cloud provider implements security is by setting baselines and minimum standards, while offering a suite of add-ons or extensions to security that typically come with an additional cost. This allows the cloud provider to support a common baseline and offer additional controls on a per-customer basis to those that require or desire them. On the other hand, for many smaller companies and organizations, who would not typically have extensive financial assets and expertise, moving to a major cloud provider may very well offer significantly enhanced security for their applications at a much lower cost than they could get on their own. In effect, they are realizing the economies of scale, and the demands of larger corporations and systems will benefit their own systems for a cheaper cost. Even the largest companies can greatly benefit, as the offerings for encryption with a cloud such as AWS far exceed what most could ever have on their own.

Privacy

Privacy in the cloud environment requires particular care due to the large number of regulatory and legal requirements that can differ greatly by use and location. Adding even more complexity is the fact that laws and regulations may differ based on where the data is stored (data at rest) and where the data is exposed and consumed (data in transit). In cloud environments, especially large public cloud systems, data has the inherent ability to be stored and moved between different locations, from within a country, between countries, and even across continents.

Cloud providers will very often have in place mechanisms to keep systems housed in geographic locations based on a customer's requirements and regulations, but it is incumbent on the Cloud Security Professional to verify and ensure that these mechanisms are functioning properly. Contractual requirements need to be clearly spelled out between the customer and cloud provider, but strict SLAs and the ability to audit compliance are also important. In particular, European countries have strict privacy regulations that a company must always be cognizant of or else face enormous penalties that many other countries do not have; the ability of the cloud provider to properly enforce location and security requirements will not protect a company from sanctions and penalties for compliance failure, because the burden resides fully on the owner of the application and the data held within.

Auditability

Most leading cloud providers supply their customers with a good deal of auditing, including reports and evidence that show user activity, compliance with controls and regulations, systems and processes that run, and an explanation of what they do, as well as information, data access, and modification records. Auditability of a cloud environment is an area where the Cloud Security Professional needs to pay particular attention because the customer does not have full control over the environment like they would in a proprietary and traditional data center model. It is up to the cloud provider to expose auditing, logs, and reports to the customer and show diligence and evidence that they are capturing all events within their environment and properly reporting them.

Governance

Governance at its core involves assigning jobs, tasks, roles, and responsibilities and ensuring they are satisfactorily performed. Whether in a traditional data center or a cloud model, governance is mostly the same and undertaken by the same approach, with a bit of added complexity in a cloud environment due to data protection requirements and the role of the cloud provider. Although the cloud environment adds complexity to governance and oversight, it also brings some benefits as well. Most cloud providers offer extensive and regular reporting and metrics, either in real time from their web portals or in the form of regular reporting. These metrics can be tuned to the cloud environment and configured in such a way so as to give an organization greater ease in verifying compliance as opposed to a traditional data center, where reporting and collection mechanisms have to be established and maintained. However, care also needs to be taken with portability and migration between different cloud providers or hosting models to ensure that metrics are equivalent or comparable to be able to maintain a consistent and ongoing governance process.

Maintenance and Versioning

With the different types of cloud service categories, it is important for the contract and SLA to clearly spell out maintenance responsibilities. With a SaaS implementation, the cloud provider is basically responsible for all upgrades, patching, and maintenance. whereas with PaaS and certainly IaaS, some duties belong to the cloud customer while the rest are retained by the cloud provider. Outlining maintenance and testing practices and timelines with the SLA is particularly important for applications that may not always work correctly because of new versions or changes to the underlying system. This requires the cloud provider and cloud customer to work out a balance between the needs of the cloud provider to maintain a uniform environment and the needs of the cloud customer to ensure continuity of operations and system stability. Whenever a system upgrade or maintenance is performed, it is crucial to establish version numbers for platforms and software. With versioning, changes can be tracked and tested, with known versions available to fall back to if necessary due to problems with new versions. There should be an overlap period where a previous version (or versions) is available, which should be spelled out in the SLA.

Reversibility

Reversibility is the ability of a cloud customer to take all their systems and data out of a cloud provider and have assurances from the cloud provider that all the data has been securely and completely removed within an agreed-upon timeline. In most cases this will be done by the cloud customer by first retrieving all their data and processes from the cloud provider, serving notice that all active and available files and systems should be deleted, and then removing all traces from long-term archives or storage at an agreed-upon point in time.

Chapter Review

This chapter gives a strong foundation of the principles and concepts that comprise a cloud infrastructure. With virtual hosting and resource allocation, cloud customers can request and allocate resources without the need to worry about underlying hardware or adding new components to systems, as they would in a traditional data center. We covered the three main types of cloud service categories that will form a major component of AWS offerings, along with the universal concepts of cloud computing.

Exercise 2-1: Creating an AWS Account

As a first exercise, we will create an AWS account. This will allow you to navigate the AWS administrative portals and will be necessary for exercises in later chapters.

1. Open your favorite web browser.

2. Go to https://aws.amazon.com.

3. Click the Create An AWS Account button in the upper-right corner.

4. Enter the requested information on the sign-up page, as shown in Figure 2-1:

   a. E-mail address

   b. Password (be sure to use a strong password!)

   c. Confirm the password

   d. AWS account name—this can be any name you desire, typically your full name, and it can be changed later from the Account Settings page

   e. Click Continue

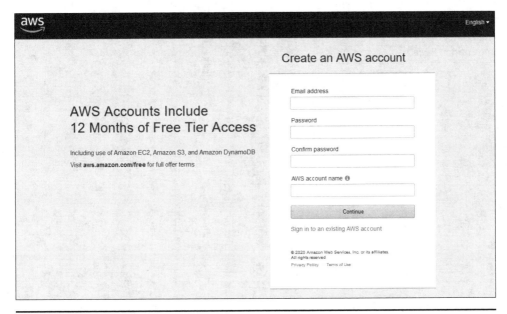

Figure 2-1 The Create An AWS Account page

5. Fill out the Contact Information Page, as shown in Figure 2-2:

    a. Choose the account type that you would like. The only difference with Professional versus Personal is the Company Name field.

    b. Fill in the pertinent contact information.

    c. Check the box to confirm the AWS Customer Agreement.

    d. Click the Create Account And Continue button.

6. Fill out the Payment Information page:

    a. Nothing will be charged to you to simply create the account, and any exercises presented in the book will not incur any charges either, as we will use the AWS Free Tier.

> **NOTE** AWS will make a $1 charge that will be reversed to verify the card is valid.

    b. Click Verify And Add.

7. Complete the Confirm Your Identity page:

    a. Enter a phone number or a mobile number to receive an SMS message.

    b. Fill out the Security Check challenge.

    c. Click Send SMS or Contact Me, depending on the method chosen.

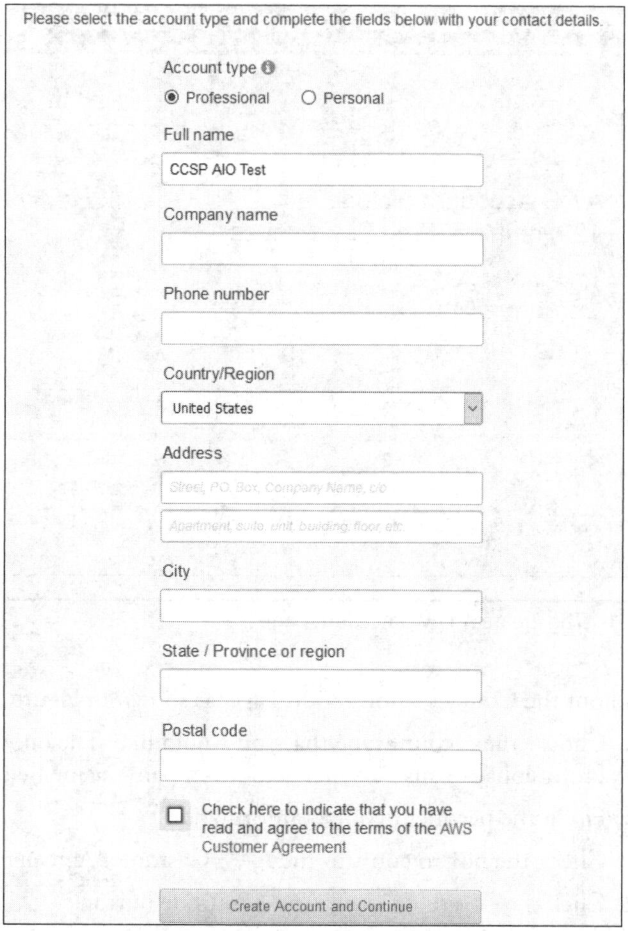

Figure 2-2
The Contact
Information Page

Please select the account type and complete the fields below with your contact details.

Account type ⓘ

◉ Professional   ○ Personal

Full name

    CCSP AIO Test

Company name

Phone number

Country/Region

    United States

Address

    Street, PO Box, Company Name, c/o

    Apartment, suite, unit, building, floor, etc.

City

State / Province or region

Postal code

☐ Check here to indicate that you have
read and agree to the terms of the AWS
Customer Agreement

Create Account and Continue

8. You will receive an SMS or a call with a code:

   a. Enter the code and click Verify.

   b. You will receive a splash screen that your identity has been verified.

   c. Click Continue.

9. You are now presented with the Select A Support Plan page:

   a. For the purposes of this book, you can select the Free basic plan. If you want to change this later or use a paid plan, that is perfectly fine, but will not be necessary for any exercises.

10. You will now receive a message that your account is being created. You will receive an e-mail when it is ready.

11. Click Sign-in To The Console.

12. Keep Root User selected and enter the e-mail address you used.

13. Click Next and enter the password you used during account creation.

14. You should now be successfully logged into the AWS Management Console!

15. You will also receive an e-mail confirmation that your account has been created and is ready to use.

16. Feel free to click around and explore the Management Console some.

Exercise 2-2: Exploring the AWS Management Console

Now that you have created an AWS account, we will do some initial exploration of the Management Console to gain some familiarity as we delve into topics in the later domains.

1. Open your favorite web browser.

2. Go to https://aws.amazon.com.

3. Hover over the My Account link in the upper right, and then select AWS Management Console from the dropdown menu.

4. Log in to your account with the root user and password that you established in the previous exercise.

5. In the upper-left corner you will see an option for Services.

   a. Click on the Services option, which will expand the menu and show you the breadth of AWS services, as shown in Figure 2-3.

6. From the expanded menu, click on the first option under Compute for EC2.

7. The EC2 services dashboard is now displayed. This shows a typical screen for AWS services that you will encounter, as shown in Figure 2-4.

8. On the EC2 dashboard, you will notice a few key displays and options:

   - In the middle of the page you will see the current Resources panel. This shows the current instances you have, as well as security groups, volumes, etc.

   - Below the Resources panel you will have the option to Launch Instance, which will take you to the wizard to create an EC2 instance.

   - Next to the Launch Instance panel you will see a readout of current service health, which displays information from the various AWS Zones and Availability Zones.

   - In the left column you will have the major options for actions you would take applicable to EC2.

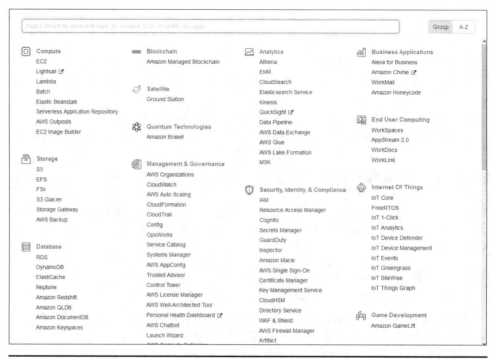

Figure 2-3   The list of services available to AWS account holders in the AWS Management Console

Figure 2-4   The AWS EC2 services dashboard

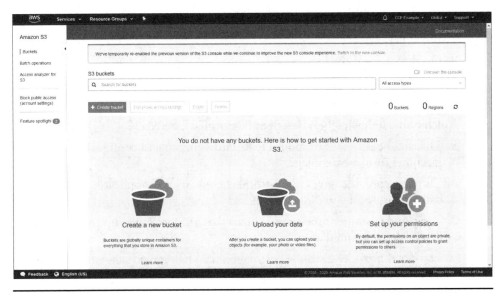

Figure 2-5 The S3 storage service Management Console screen

9. Expand the Services tab on the upper right, and this time, under Storage select S3.

10. This will display the S3 storage service. You will see that you do not have any buckets currently configured, but you will be presented with menus to create a new bucket, upload data, or set permissions, as shown in Figure 2-5.

11. Feel free to click through many of the services from the Services tab to gain some familiarity with how the screens look for each one. This will also give you some beginning familiarity with the names of the AWS services and what type of services they are, such as compute, storage, database, etc.

Questions

1. Which of the following best describes interoperability?

    A. Systems that work with any client software and access methods

    B. Systems that will work with any type of network offerings

    C. Systems that operate independently of particular platforms and hosting providers

    D. Systems that are compatible with most operating systems and mobile devices

2. Which cloud deployment model best characterizes AWS?

    A. Private

    B. Public

    C. Hybrid

    D. Community

3. Which of the following is most pertinent to cost-saving benefits of cloud computing?

   A. Broad network access

   B. On-demand self-service

   C. Resource pooling

   D. Metered service

4. Which of the following best describes Platform as a Service?

   A. The cloud customer is responsible for provisioning and configuring virtual machines from a base image.

   B. The cloud provider gives the customer access to a full application where only data imports and branding are required.

   C. The cloud customer provisions systems that are configured up to the point of deploying code and data.

   D. The cloud provider gives the customer a fully configured network, but the customer is responsible for the configuration of all virtual machines within it.

5. Which cloud concept would most interest a company that wants flexibility in choosing different cloud providers as their needs change?

   A. Reversibility

   B. Availability

   C. Resiliency

   D. Portability

6. Which of the following best fits the responsibility of the cloud customer with a Software as a Service application?

   A. A cloud customer provisions virtual machines that have a base image and just require software installation specific to their needs.

   B. The cloud customer gains access to a fully featured application that just requires their user data and access, possibly with branding also allowed.

   C. The cloud provider allocates fully built systems that require a customer to integrate their custom application code.

   D. A cloud provider gives access to a vast software suite of utilities and libraries that a customer can access as needed for their own deployments.

7. Which of the following best describes scalability?

   A. A customer only pays for the resources they need and are using at a particular time.

   B. The ability to deploy as many virtual machines as a cloud customer requires.

   C. The ability to statically change the level of computing or storage resources to meet changing demands.

   D. Having unlimited resources within a cloud infrastructure.

8. Which cloud deployment model is often used in conjunction with a company's disaster recovery plan?

   A. Public

   B. Hybrid

   C. Community

   D. Private

9. Which of the following situations would most benefit a company's costs by utilizing cloud computing?

   A. A healthcare company experiences a significant increase in utilization during the annual open enrollment period.

   B. A company has consistent utilization through the year without many bursts or down periods.

   C. A sports news system gets a 50 percent increase in traffic on weekends versus weekdays.

   D. A publishing company gets short, sporadic bursts of traffic with news items.

10. Which of the following best describes Infrastructure as a Service?

   A. The cloud customer is responsible for provisioning and configuring virtual machines from a base image.

   B. The cloud provider gives the customer access to a full application where only data imports and branding are required.

   C. The cloud customer provisions systems that are configured up to the point of deploying code and data.

   D. The cloud provider gives the customer a fully configured network, but the customer is responsible for the configuration of all virtual machines within it.

Questions and Answers

1. Which of the following best describes interoperability?

   A. Systems that work with any client software and access methods

   B. Systems that will work with any type of network offerings

   C. Systems that operate independently of particular platforms and hosting providers

   D. Systems that are compatible with most operating systems and mobile devices

   ☑ C. Interoperability pertains to the ability of a system to reuse components and services, without being dependent on a particular hosting provider. This allows systems to easily move between cloud providers and maintains the most flexibility and options for a company.

2. Which cloud deployment model best characterizes AWS?

   A. Private

   B. Public

   C. Hybrid

   D. Community

   ☑ **B.** AWS utilizes a public cloud deployment model where anyone can sign up for an account and allocate resources, with the limitations applying to their finances and resources.

3. Which of the following is most pertinent to cost-saving benefits of cloud computing?

   A. Broad network access

   B. On-demand self-service

   C. Resource pooling

   D. Metered service

   ☑ **D.** Metered service allows a company to only pay for resources during the time they are actually allocated and in use. This allows a company to alter their resources as needed and to disable during times of nonuse, versus a traditional data center, where hardware must be purchased and active, whether it is actually being used or not.

4. Which of the following best describes Platform as a Service?

   A. The cloud customer is responsible for provisioning and configuring virtual machines from a base image.

   B. The cloud provider gives the customer access to a full application where only data imports and branding are required.

   C. The cloud customer provisions systems that are configured up to the point of deploying code and data.

   D. The cloud provider gives the customer a fully configured network, but the customer is responsible for the configuration of all virtual machines within it.

   ☑ **C.** With Platform as a Service, the cloud provider provisions fully built systems that have all necessary libraries and software platforms that a customer can quickly deploy their code and data on to begin utilization.

5. Which cloud concept would most interest a company that wants flexibility in choosing different cloud providers as their needs change?

    A. Reversibility

    B. Availability

    C. Resiliency

    D. Portability

    ☑ **D.** Portability pertains to the ability of a company to quickly and easily move systems between cloud providers. This is maintained by minimizing the utilization of proprietary offerings from cloud providers that would be unique to that provider and would prevent their easy move to a different offering.

6. Which of the following best fits the responsibility of the cloud customer with a Software as a Service application?

    A. A cloud customer provisions virtual machines that have a base image and just require software installation specific to their needs.

    B. The cloud customer gains access to a fully featured application that just requires their user data and access, possibly with branding also allowed.

    C. The cloud provider allocates fully built systems that require a customer to integrate their custom application code.

    D. A cloud provider gives access to a vast software suite of utilities and libraries that a customer can access as needed for their own deployments.

    ☑ **B.** With Software as a Service, a customer contracts for a fully built and ready software application. The customer typically will need to provision user access and user data, along with possibly branding with their own logos and text. The application is fully maintained by the cloud provider, and a customer does not have the ability to modify code.

7. Which of the following best describes scalability?

    A. A customer only pays for the resources they need and are using at a particular time.

    B. The ability to deploy as many virtual machines as a cloud customer requires.

    C. The ability to statically change the level of computing or storage resources to meet changing demands.

    D. Having unlimited resources within a cloud infrastructure.

    ☑ **C.** Scalability pertains to the ability to change the level of resources being utilized by a cloud customer to meet current demands over time. This includes both the ability to add resources for new deployments or expected needs and the ability to downgrade resources and save costs when not needed.

8. Which cloud deployment model is often used in conjunction with a company's disaster recovery plan?

   A. Public

   B. Hybrid

   C. Community

   D. Private

   ☑ **B.** Hybrid cloud environments, which use a mix of traditional data centers with the cloud or utilize multiple cloud models, are often used as a backup and standby platform for a company's disaster recovery plans.

9. Which of the following situations would most benefit a company's costs by utilizing cloud computing?

   A. A healthcare company experiences a significant increase in utilization during the annual open enrollment period.

   B. A company has consistent utilization through the year without many bursts or down periods.

   C. A sports news system gets a 50 percent increase in traffic on weekends versus weekdays.

   D. A publishing company gets short, sporadic bursts of traffic with news items.

   ☑ **A.** With a defined period of high utilization of a cyclical nature, a healthcare company could save significant costs with cloud computing, where resources can be increased during those peak periods and otherwise operate at a much lower level the majority of the year.

10. Which of the following best describes Infrastructure as a Service?

    A. The cloud customer is responsible for provisioning and configuring virtual machines from a base image.

    B. The cloud provider gives the customer access to a full application where only data imports and branding are required.

    C. The cloud customer provisions systems that are configured up to the point of deploying code and data.

    D. The cloud provider gives the customer a fully configured network, but the customer is responsible for the configuration of all virtual machines within it.

    ☑ **D.** With Infrastructure as a Service, the cloud provider gives the customer a base environment where they can fully deploy virtual machines and virtual network devices. The cloud customer is responsible for all deployments and configurations beyond the base environment.

Security and Compliance

In this chapter, you will learn the following Domain 2 topics:
- Define the AWS Shared Responsibility Model
- Define AWS Cloud security and compliance concepts
- Identify AWS access management capabilities
- Identity resources for security support

Security is a primary focus for AWS across all services and one of the most prominent benefits of using a cloud provider. AWS can implement extremely robust security through economies of scale that can far exceed what any organization could have the finances and experience to implement on their own. This domain will introduce you to the Shared Responsibility Model that cloud providers employ, as well as the key concepts used with cloud security. We will cover the specific implementations of these concepts by AWS and the resources available to users for security support.

The AWS Shared Responsibility Model

Any large and complex IT system is built upon multiple layers of services and components, and a cloud is certainly a prime example of that model.

Underlying Cloud Framework

With any cloud offering, the underlying infrastructure is the sole responsibility of the cloud provider. This includes everything from the physical building and facilities to the power infrastructure and redundancy, physical security, and network cabling and hardware components. This also includes the underlying computing infrastructure such as hypervisors, CPU, memory, and storage. Within the AWS infrastructure, the responsibility for regions, availability zones, and edge locations is solely the responsibility of AWS.

However, beyond the layers of physical facilities and computing hardware, there are differing levels of responsibility based upon the cloud services model employed. Table 3-1 shows the areas of responsibility within a cloud implementation. The shaded areas represent the responsibility on the part of the cloud provider.

IaaS	PaaS	SaaS
Data	Data	Data
Application Code	Application Code	Application Code
Database	Database	Database
OS	OS	OS
Virtualization	Virtualization	Virtualization
Networking	Networking	Networking
Storage	Storage	Storage
Hardware	Hardware	Hardware

Table 3-1 Areas of Responsibility

 EXAM TIP Make sure to understand the Shared Responsibility Model and what the customer is responsible for in each service category. This will play a prominent role throughout the discussion on the AWS service offerings.

IaaS

With Infrastructure as a Service (IaaS), the customer is responsible for everything beginning with the operating system. The cloud provider is responsible for the underlying host infrastructure from which the customer can deploy virtual devices into, whether they are virtual machines or virtual networking components. After that, responsibility is very similar to a traditional data center, in which the administrators are responsible for virtual machines and all software, code, and data within them.

PaaS

With Platform as a Service (PaaS), the cloud provider is responsible for an entire hosting platform, including all software, libraries, and middleware that the customer needs. The customer then deploys their application code and data into the environment. This is most heavily used for DevOps, where developers can quickly obtain fully featured hosting environments and only need to deploy their code and any needed data to test and develop with, and do not need to worry about any underlying operating system or middleware issues.

SaaS

With Software as a Service (SaaS), the cloud provider is responsible for everything except specific customer or user data. SaaS is a fully featured application that a customer only needs to load users or do minimal configuration, along with possibly importing data about customers or services. This model has the least level of responsibility for the customer, but as such, also typically comes with the highest costs of service.

Managed vs. Unmanaged

A major question for any customer is whether to use managed or unmanaged resources within a cloud environment. While both can ultimately provide what is needed to meet the business needs of the customer, there are pros and cons of each approach.

Managed resources are those where the cloud provider is responsible for the installation, patching, maintenance, and security of a resource. On the inverse, unmanaged resources are those hosted within a cloud environment, but where the customer bears responsibility for host functions. Managed resources will typically cost more directly than unmanaged resources, as the customer is paying for a premium service and the cloud provider is responsible for all of the maintenance and monitoring of the service. However, while managed resources may appear to cost more up-front, once an organization factors in all the staff time to perform the same level of responsibilities, as well as the included costs of responsibility for monitoring and uptime, managed resources almost always represent an enormous benefit to the cloud customer overall.

A prime example relating to managed versus unmanaged is with a database. A customer could opt, for example, to provision a virtual machine and install a database such as MySQL or Microsoft SQL Server on it. While this would give the customer full control over the database, it would also place the burden for all configurations, security, and patches onto the cloud customer. The customer could instead opt to use the Relational Database Service (RDS) that is offered by AWS. Going this route would leave the customer only with the responsibility of loading their data into RDS and would transfer the burden for maintenance and security to AWS, allowing the customer to more fully focus on their business operations and not on system administration.

Regulatory Compliance

If your application utilizes or stores any type of sensitive information, there will be specific regulatory requirements that you will need to ensure compliance with. This type of data can range from credit card and financial information to health records, academic records, or government systems and data. Each type of data will have specific laws and regulations for how the data must be handled and protected, governed by the jurisdiction that your systems are subject to.

To assist with meeting regulatory requirements, AWS offers their Artifact service, which can be accessed directly from the AWS Management Console that you already established an account for in the last chapter. This is included as a service with all AWS accounts and does not require additional costs or services.

As part of the Artifact service, AWS undergoes certification reviews and audits by various governing bodies. This includes prominent certifications such as PCI-DSS for financial/credit card transactions and FedRAMP for U.S. federal government systems. AWS also makes the pertinent Service Organization Controls (SOC) audit reports available to customers.

An additional feature that AWS offers through Artifact is enabling a customer to review and accept agreements for their individual account and what they need to maintain compliance with, along with terminating the agreement if no longer needed.

Data Security

Several toolsets and technologies are commonly used as data security strategies:

- Encryption
- Key management
- Masking
- Obfuscation
- Anonymization
- Tokenization

These range from the encryption of data to prevent unauthorized access to the masking and tokenization of data to render it protected in the event that it is leaked or accessed.

Encryption

With the concepts of multitenancy and resource pooling being central to any cloud environment, the use of encryption to protect data is essential and required, as the typical protections of physical separation and segregation found in a traditional data center model are not available or applicable to a cloud environment. The architecture of an encryption system has three basic components: the data itself, the encryption engine that handles all the encryption activities, and the encryption keys used in the actual encryption and use of the data.

There are many different types and levels of encryption. Within a cloud environment, it is the duty of the organization to evaluate the needs of the application, the technologies it employs, the types of data it contains, and the regulatory or contractual requirements for its protection and use. Encryption is important for many aspects of a cloud implementation. This includes the storage of data on a system, both when it is being accessed and while it is at rest, as well as the actual transmission of data and transactions between systems or between the system and a consumer. The organization must ensure that appropriate encryption is selected that will be strong enough to meet regulatory and system requirements but also efficient and accessible enough for operations to seamlessly work within the application.

Data in Transit

Data in transit is the state of data when it is actually being used by an application and is traversing systems internally or going between the client and the actual application. Whether the data is being transmitted between systems within the cloud or going out to a user's client, data in transit is when data is most vulnerable to exposure of unauthorized capture. Within a cloud hosting model, the transmission between systems is even more important than with a traditional data center due to multitenancy; the other systems within the same cloud are potential security risks and vulnerable points where data capture could happen successfully.

In order to maintain portability and interoperability, the Cloud Security Professional should make the processes for the encryption of data in transit vendor-neutral in regard to the capabilities or limitations of a specific cloud provider. The Cloud Security Professional should be involved in the planning and design of the system or application from the earliest stages to ensure that everything is built properly from the ground up and not retrofitted after design or implementation has been completed. Whereas the use of encryption with the operations of the system is crucial during the design phase, the proper management of keys, protocols, and testing/auditing is crucial once a system has been implemented and deployed.

The most common method for data-in-transit encryption is to use the well-known SSL and TLS technologies under HTTPS. With many modern applications utilizing web services as the framework for communications, this has become the prevailing method, which is the same method used by clients and browsers to communicate with servers over the Internet. This method is now being used within cloud environments for server-to-server internal communication as well. Beyond using HTTPS, other common encryption methods for data in transit are VPNs (virtual private networks) and IPsec. These methods can be used by themselves but are most commonly used in parallel to provide the highest level of protection possible.

Data at Rest

Data at rest refers to information stored on a system or device (versus data that is actively being transmitted across a network or between systems). The data can be stored in many different forms to fit within this category. Some examples include databases, file sets, spreadsheets, documents, tapes, archives, and even mobile devices.

Data residing on a system is potentially exposed and vulnerable far longer than short transmission and transaction operations would be, so special care is needed to ensure its protection from unauthorized access. With transaction systems and data in transit, usually a small subset of records or even a single record is transmitted at any time, versus the comprehensive record sets maintained in databases and other file systems.

While encrypting data is central to the confidentiality of any system, the availability and performance of data are equally as important. The Cloud Security Professional must ensure that encryption methods provide high levels of security and protection and do so in a manner that facilitates high performance and system speed. Any use of encryption will cause higher load and processing times, so proper scaling and evaluation of systems are critical when testing deployments and design criteria.

With portability and vendor lock-in considerations, it is important for a Cloud Security Professional to ensure that encryption systems do not effectively cause a system to be bound to a proprietary cloud offering. If a system or application ends up using a proprietary encryption system from a cloud provider, portability will likely be far more difficult and thus tie that customer to that particular cloud provider. With many cloud implementations spanning multiple cloud providers and infrastructures for disaster recovery and continuity planning, having encryption systems that can maintain consistency and performance is important.

EXAM TIP Data-at-rest encryption and security are very important in a cloud environment due to the reliance on virtual machines. In a traditional data center, you can have systems that are powered off and inaccessible. In a virtual environment, when a system is not powered on or started, the disk and memory are gone, but the underlying image still exists within storage and carries a possibility of compromise or corruption, especially if a developer has stored application or customer data on the VM image.

Encryption with Data States

Encryption is used in various manners and through different technology approaches, depending on the state of the data at the time—in use, at rest, or in motion. With data in use, the data is being actively accessed and processed. Because this process is the most removed from and independent of the host system, technologies such as data rights management (DRM) and information rights management (IRM) are the most capable and mature approaches that can be taken at this time (both are discussed in depth later in this chapter). Data in transit pertains to the active transmission of data across the network, and as such, the typical security protocols and technologies employed are available within a cloud environment (for example, TLS/SSL, VPN, IPsec, and HTTPS). With data at rest, where the data is sitting idle within the environment and storage systems, file-level and storage-level encryption mechanisms will be employed, depending on the location and state of the data; files sitting on a file system versus in a database or other storage architecture will likely require different types of encryption engines and technologies to secure them based on the particular needs and requirements of the system employed. The Cloud Security Professional must pay particular attention to any specific regulatory requirements for the classification of the data under consideration and ensure that the encryption methods chosen satisfy the minimums of all applicable standards and laws.

Challenges with Encryption

There is a myriad of challenges with implementing encryption. Some are applicable no matter where the data is housed, and others are specific issues to cloud environments. A central challenge to encryption implementations is the dependence on key sets to handle the actual encryption and decryption processes. Without the proper security of encryption keys, or exposure to external parties such as the cloud provider itself, the entire encryption scheme could be rendered vulnerable and insecure. (More on the specific issues with key management will follow in the next section.) With any software-based encryption scheme, core computing components such as processor and memory are vital, and within a cloud environment specifically, these components are shared across all the hosted customers. This can make resources such as memory vulnerable to exposure and could thus compromise the implementation of the encryption operations. It can also be a challenge implementing encryption throughout applications that are moving into a cloud hosting environment that were not designed initially to engage with encryption systems, from both a technical and performance capacity, because code changes or unacceptable levels of performance degradation may become apparent with the integration of encryption. As a last major concern, encryption does not ensure data integrity, only confidentiality within an environment. Additional steps will need to be integrated for those environments where integrity is a pressing concern.

Encryption Implementations

The actual implementation of encryption and how it is applied will depend largely on the type of storage being used within the cloud environment.

With database storage systems, two layers of encryption are typically applied and available. First, database systems will reside on volume storage systems, resembling a typical file system of a server model. The actual database files can be protected through encryption methods at the file system level; this also serves to protect the data at rest. Within the database system itself are encryption methods that can be applied to the data set, either wholesale or on a granular level, by encrypting specific tables or columns of data. This type of encryption can be handled by the database application itself or by the actual software application that handles the encryption and stores the data in that state.

For object storage, apart from the encryption at the actual file level, which is handled by the cloud provider, encryption can be used within the application itself. The most prevalent means for this is through IRM technologies or via encryption within the applicant itself. With IRM, which will be covered later in this chapter, encryption can be applied to the objects to control their usage after they have left the system. With application-level encryption, the application effectively acts as a proxy between the user and the object storage and ensures encryption during the transaction. However, once the object has left the application framework, no protection is provided.

Lastly, with volume storage, many of the typical encryption systems used on a traditional server model can be employed within a cloud framework. This encryption is most useful with data-at-rest scenarios. Due to the application itself being able to read the encrypted data on the volume, any compromise of the application will render the file system encryption ineffective when it comes to protecting the data.

Hashing

Hashing involves taking data of arbitrary type, length, or size and using a function to map a value that is of a fixed size. Hashing can be applied to virtually any type of data object, including text strings, documents, images, binary data, and even virtual machine images.

The main value of hashing is to quickly verify the integrity of data objects. Within a cloud environment this can offer great value with virtual machine images and the potentially large number of data locations within a dispersed environment. As many copies of a file are potentially stored in many different locations, hashing can be used to very quickly verify that the files are of identical composure and that the integrity of them has not been compromised. Hashes are widely used in a similar fashion by vendors, and especially open-source software distributions, to enable an administrator to verify they have not been compromised in some manager on a mirror site and that the file is a pure copy of the actual distribution by the publisher. This process is widely referred to by common terms such as checksums, digests, or fingerprints.

A large variety of hashing functions are commonly used and supported. The vast majority of users will have no problem using any of the freely and widely available options, which will suit their needs for data integrity and comparison without issue. There is also the option for any organization to implement their own hashing systems or seeding with their own values for their specific internal purposes. Whether a freely available hashing function is used or if an organization opts to use their own internal processes, the overall operation and value are the same.

Key Management

Key management is the safeguarding of encryption keys and the access to them. Within a cloud environment, key management is an essential and highly important task, while also being very complex. It is one of the most important facets of cloud hosting for the Cloud Security Professional to focus on at all times.

One of the most important security considerations with key management is the access to the keys and the storage of them. Access to keys in any environment is extremely important and critical to security, but in a cloud environment, where you have multitenancy and the cloud provider personnel having broad administrative access to systems, there are more considerations than in a traditional data center concerning the segregation and control of the staff of the customer. Of course, there can also be a big difference in key management between IaaS and PaaS implementations, as well as the level of involvement and access that the cloud provider's staff will need to have. Where the keys are stored is also an important consideration within a cloud environment. In a traditional data center configuration, the key management system will typically be on dedicated hardware and systems, segregated from the rest of the environment. Within a cloud environment, due to multitenancy, protection of the virtual machine hosting the key management system is vital. The use of encryption is crucial to prevent any unauthorized access. The Cloud Security Professional will always need to consult with applicable regulatory concerns for any key management, access, and storage requirements and determine whether a cloud provider can meet those requirements.

No matter what hosting model is used by an organization, a few principles of key management are important. Key management should always be performed only on trusted systems and by trusted processes, whether in a traditional data center or a cloud environment. In a cloud environment, careful consideration must be given to the level of trust that can be established within the environment of the cloud provider and whether that will meet management and regulatory requirements. Although confidentiality and security are always the top concerns with key management, in a cloud environment, where heavy use of encryption throughout the entire system is paramount, the issue of the availability of the key management system is also of central importance. If the key management system were to become unavailable, essentially the entire system and applications would also become unavailable for the duration of the outage. One way to mitigate the possibility of cloud provider staff having access to the keys used within the environment is to host the key management system outside of the cloud provider. Although this will certainly attain the segregation of duties and provide higher security in regard to that one specific area, it also increases the complexity of the system overall and introduces the same availability concerns. In other words, if the externally hosted key management system becomes unavailable or inaccessible, even if caused by something as mundane as an inadvertent firewall or ACL change, the entire system will be inaccessible.

Key storage can be implemented in a cloud environment in three ways. The first is internal storage, where the keys are stored and accessed within the same virtual machine as the encryption service or engine. Internal storage is the simplest implementation—it keeps the entire process together, and it is appropriate for some storage types such as database and backup system encryption. However, it also ties the system and keys closely together, and compromise of the system overall can lead to potential key compromise— although it does alleviate the external availability and connection problems. The second method is external storage, where the keys are maintained separately from the systems and security processes (such as encryption). The external hosting can be anywhere so long as it is not on the same system performing the encryption functions, so typically this would be a dedicated host within the same environment, but it could be completely external. In this type of implementation, the availability aspect is important. The third method involves having an external and independent service or system host the key storage. This will typically increase security precautions and safeguards in a widely accepted manner because the key storage is handled by an organization dedicated to that specific task that maintains systems specifically scoped for that function, with well-documented security configurations, policies, and operations.

Tokenization

Tokenization is the practice of utilizing a random and opaque "token" value in data to replace what otherwise would be a sensitive or protected data object. The token value is usually generated by the application with a means to map it back to the actual real value, and then the token value is placed in the data set with the same formatting and requirements of the actual real value, so that the application can continue to function without different modifications or code changes. Tokenization represents a way for an organization to remove sensitive data from an application without having to introduce more intensive processes such as encryption to meet regulatory or policy requirements. As with any technology used to complement an application, especially in regard to data security, the system and processes used for tokenization will need to be properly secured. Failure to implement proper controls with the tokenization process will lead to the same vulnerabilities and problems as insecure key management with encryption or other data safeguard failures. The tokenization process provided on behalf of the cloud provider should be carefully vetted, both to ensure the security and governance of it and to limit any possibility of vendor lock-in.

Data Loss Prevention

A major concept and approach employed in a cloud environment to protect data is known as *data loss prevention* (DLP), or sometimes as *data leakage prevention*. DLP is a set of controls and practices put in place to ensure that data is only accessible and exposed to those users and systems authorized to have it. The goals of a DLP strategy for an organization are to manage and minimize risk, maintain compliance with regulatory requirements, and show due diligence on the part of the application and data owner. However, it is vital for any organization to take a holistic view of DLP and not focus on individual systems or hosting environments. The DLP strategy should involve their entire enterprise, particularly with hybrid cloud environments, or those where there is a combination of cloud and traditional data center installations.

DLP Components

Any DLP implementation is composed of three common components: discovery and classification, monitoring, and enforcement.

The discovery and classification stage is the first stage of the DLP implementation; it is focused on the actual finding of data that is pertinent to the DLP strategy, ensuring that all instances of it are known and able to be exposed to the DLP solution, and determining the security classification and requirements of the data once it has been found. This also allows the matching of data within the environment to any regulatory requirements for its protection and assurance.

Once data has been discovered and classified, it can then be monitored with DLP implementations. The monitoring stage encompasses the core function and purpose of a DLP strategy. It involves the actual process of watching data as it moves through the various states of usage to ensure it is being used in appropriate and controlled ways. It also ensures that those who access and use the data are authorized to do so and are using it in an appropriate manner.

The final stage of a DLP implementation is the actual enforcement of policies and any potential violations caught as part of the monitoring stage. If any potential violations are detected by the DLP implementation, a variety of measures can be automatically taken, depending on the policies set forth by management. This can range from simply logging and alerting of a potential violation to actually blocking and stopping the potential violation when it is first detected.

DLP Data States

With data at rest (DAR), the DLP solution is installed on the systems holding the data, which can be servers, desktops, workstations, or mobile devices. In many instances, this will involve archived data and long-term storage data. This is the simplest DLP solution to deploy throughout the enterprise overall but might also require network integration to be the most effective.

With data in transit (DIT), the DLP solution is deployed near the network perimeter to capture traffic as it leaves the network through various protocols, such as HTTP/HTTPS and SMTP. It looks for data that is leaving or attempting to leave the area that does not conform to security policies, either in subject or in format. One thing to note: if the traffic leaving the environment is encrypted, the DLP solution will need to be able to read and process the encrypted traffic in order to function, which might require key management and encryption aspects coming into play.

Lastly, with data in use (DIU), the DLP solution is deployed on the users' workstations or devices in order to monitor the data access and use from the endpoint.

The biggest challenges with this type of implementation are reach and the complexity of having all access points covered. This can be especially true within a cloud environment where users are geographically dispersed and use a large variety of clients to access the systems and applications.

 CAUTION DLP on end-user devices can be a particular challenge for any cloud application. Because it requires the end user to install an application or plug-in to work, you will need to make sure you fully understand the types of devices your users will be utilizing, as well as any costs and requirements associated with the use of the technology. The growth of "bring your own device" (BYOD) within many organizations will also have a profound impact on any DLP strategies and should be reflected in policies.

DLP Cloud Implementations and Practices

The cloud environment brings additional challenges to DLP, much like any other type of implementation or policy, when compared to those challenges in a traditional data center. The biggest difference/challenge is in the way cloud environments store data. Data in a cloud is spread across large storage systems, with varying degrees of replication and redundancy, and oftentimes where the data will be stored and accessed is unpredictable. For a DLP strategy, this can pose a particular challenge because it makes properly discovering and monitoring all data used by a system or application more difficult, especially because the data can change locations over time, effectively becoming a moving target. With a cloud system using metered resource cost models and DLP adding load and resource consumption to the system, the potential for higher costs above and beyond the costs of the DLP solution is a real concern.

Data De-identification

Data de-identification involves using masking, obfuscation, or anonymization. The theory behind masking or obfuscation is to replace, hide, or remove sensitive data from data sets. The most common use for masking is making available test data sets for nonproduction and development environments. By replacing sensitive data fields with random or substituted data, these nonproduction environments can quickly utilize data sets that are similar to production for testing and development, without exposing sensitive information to systems with fewer security controls and less oversight. Many regulatory systems and industry certification programs have requirements to not use sensitive or real data in nonproduction environments, and masking is often the easiest and best way to meet such a requirement.

Typically masking is accomplished either by entirely replacing the value with a new one or by adding characters to a data field. This can be done wholesale on the entire field or just portions of it. For example, many times with credit card fields, as most who have ever purchased anything online can attest, the entire credit card number will be masked with a character such as an asterisk, but the last four digits will be left visible for identification and confirmation. Another common method is to shift values, either with the entire data set or with specific values within a field based on an algorithm, which can be done from a random or predetermined perspective. The last major method is to delete the data wholesale or just parts of the data from a field or to replace the data with overwritten null pointers or values.

The two primary strategies or methods for masking are static masking and dynamic masking. With static masking, a separate and distinct copy of the data set is created with masking in place. This is typically done through a script or other process that will take a standard data set, process it to mask the appropriate and predefined fields, and then output the data set as a new one with the completed masking done. The static method is most appropriate for data sets that are created for nonproduction environments, where testing is necessary or desired and having a data set very similar in size and structure to production is paramount. This allows testing to be done without exposing sensitive data to these environments or to developers. With dynamic masking, production environments are protected by the masking process being implemented between the application and data layers of the application. This allows for a masking translation to take place live in the system and during normal application processing of data.

 NOTE Dynamic masking is usually done where a system needs to have full and unmasked data but certain users should not have the same level of access. An example from my own personal experience is healthcare data, where the back-end system needs to have the full data, but users such as enrollment assistants and customer service representatives only need a subset of the data, or just enough of a data field to be able to verify codes or personal information without seeing the entire field of data.

With data anonymization, data is manipulated in a way to prevent the identification of an individual through various data objects. It's often used in conjunction with other concepts such as masking. Data generally has direct and indirect identifiers, with direct identifiers being the actual personal and private data, and indirect identifiers being attributes such as demographic and location data that, when used together, could lead to the identity of the individual. Data anonymization is the process of removing the indirect identifiers to prevent such an identification from taking place.

AWS Identity and Access Management

In the first chapter's exercise, you created an AWS account, which will serve as your root account. The root account has full access to all resources under your purview, and as such, must be properly protected, along with the use of other best practices for account access and security.

AWS Root Account

Just like a root account on a computer system, the AWS root account has full access to everything under your account. It can create users, provision resources, and incur financial obligations for any activities that are done with it. As with superuser accounts on any computer system, it is a best practice to not use the root account unless absolutely necessary, but instead to provision accounts that have more limited access, as well as accountability, if you have multiple users operating within the same AWS account. Along with the creation of user (IAM) accounts, the root user should be secured with a very strong and complex password, as well as the utilization of other security tools such as multifactor authentication (MFA).

The AWS IAM Dashboard

The AWS IAM dashboard can be found at https://console.aws.amazon.com/iam. You can log into this address using the same e-mail address and password that you established for your root account in the exercise from Chapter 2.

As you have just created this account, minimal security configurations and policies are applied to it at this time. When you first log in, you will see the security status of your account and the remaining steps you need to take for securing it, as shown in Figure 3-1.

Securing the Root User

When you created your root account in the first exercise, you established a password for it. This password is what you will use to access the AWS Console when using the root account. While all accounts should have a strong password, it is extra imperative for the root account to do so. Along with a strong password, MFA will add another layer of security to the account, should the password either get disclosed or compromised in some manner.

Figure 3-1
The initial status on the IAM dashboard shows the remaining steps necessary to properly secure your account.

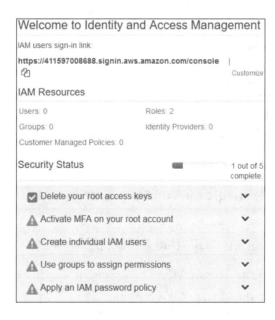

Multifactor Authentication

MFA, as its main principle, extends traditional authentication models beyond the system username and password combination to require additional factors and steps to provide for more protection and assurance as to the entity's identity and their specific sensitive information.

With a traditional authentication system, an entity provides a username and password combination to prove their identity and uniqueness. While this system provides a basic level of security and assurance, it also greatly opens the possibilities of compromise, as both pieces of information can be easily obtained or possibly guessed based on information about the user, and once possessed can be easily used by a malicious actor until either changed or detected. In particular, many people will use the same username, or use their e-mail address as their username with systems where this is allowed, thus giving a malicious actor immediate knowledge of half of the information needed to authenticate. Also, out of habit, people use the same password for many different systems, opening up a grave possibility where a compromise of one system with lower security could ultimately lead to the compromise of a more secure system for which the individual happens to use the same password.

With MFA systems, the traditional username and password scheme is expanded to include a second factor that is not simply a piece of knowledge that a malicious actor could possibly obtain or compromise. A multifactor system combines at least two different requirements, the first of which is typically a password, but doesn't need to be. Here are the three main components, of which at least two different components are required:

- **Something the user knows** This component is almost exclusively a password or a protected piece of information that in effect serves the same purpose as a password.

- **Something the user possesses** This component is something that is physically possessed by the individual. This could be a USB thumb drive, an RFID chip card, an access card with a magnetic stripe, an RSA token with a changing access code, a text message code sent to the user's mobile device, or anything else along the same lines.

- **Something the user is** This component uses biometrics, such as retina scans, palm prints, fingerprints, and so on.

Exercise 3-1: Enable MFA on Your Root Account

Let's go ahead and enable MFA on your root account to establish increased security. You should be on the IAM dashboard at this time.

1. Click on the Activate MFA On Your Root Account option.

2. Click on the Manage MFA button.

3. You will now be on the Security Credentials page. Click on the Multi-Factor Authentication (MFA) option.

4. Click on the Activate MFA button.

    a. You will now be given three options for what to use for MFA:

- **Virtual MFA Device**   This is an app installed on your smartphone, such as Authy, the Microsoft Authenticator, Google Authenticator, etc.
- **U2F Security Key**   This uses a U2F-compliant device, such as Yubikey.
- **Other Hardware MFA Device**   This requires the use of a hardware token such as those from Gemalto.

    b. For our purposes here, please install one of the smartphone apps listed earlier that are freely available for both iPhone and Android. If you already have one on your smartphone, there is no need to get another—we can use that one.

    c. With the radio button selected for Virtual MFA Device, click Continue.

    d. You will now be on the Set Up Virtual MFA Device screen.

        i. A link is provided to a list of compatible smartphone apps.

- For our purposes here, please install one of the smartphone apps listed earlier that are freely available for both iPhone and Android. If you already have one on your smartphone, there is no need to get another—we can use that one.

        ii. Click on the middle box to Show QR Code.

- Use the application you installed to scan the QR code.

        iii. The application will now display codes that will rotate every 30 seconds.

            1. You will need to enter the codes from two consecutive cycles in order to validate your MFA setup.

            2. After you enter in both, click Active, and you will see the confirmation screen.

5. On the left menu, click the Dashboard button to return to the main page.

    a. You will now see that "Activate MFA on your root account" is showing with a green checkmark as having been successfully completed.

    b. You will also notice on your MFA app that the new setup shows up as a root account.

IAM Users and Security

After securing your root account, the next step will be to create IAM users and properly secure them as well.

IAM Users Password Policies

As with any account, the first line of security is the traditional password. In order to have a credible sense of security from password authentication alone, a proper password policy must be enforced. This will prevent easily guessable or breakable passwords from being used by your IAM users.

What you ultimately use for a password policy can depend on several factors. Many best practices are available for requiring passwords of sufficient complexity that you can leverage if you have no specific requirements. In many instances, if you are representing a company or organization, you will already have password requirements that you must adhere to. Additionally, if you are using any data that falls under special regulatory requirements, you may have specific password policies related to those as well. Before you set a password policy for your IAM users, make sure you understand what specific requirements you have for your circumstances.

Exercise 3-2: Create a Password Policy for IAM Users

1. If you are not already there, log into the IAM console at https://console.aws.amazon.com/iam.

2. When you log in this time with your root account, you will have to use the MFA that you previously set up, along with your root account password.

3. On the Security Status menu, click on Apply An IAM Password Policy and then click on Manage Password Policy.

4. At the top of the Password Policy screen, click on Set Password Policy.

5. You will now be presented the options for configuring the password policy for your IAM users, as shown in Figure 3-2.

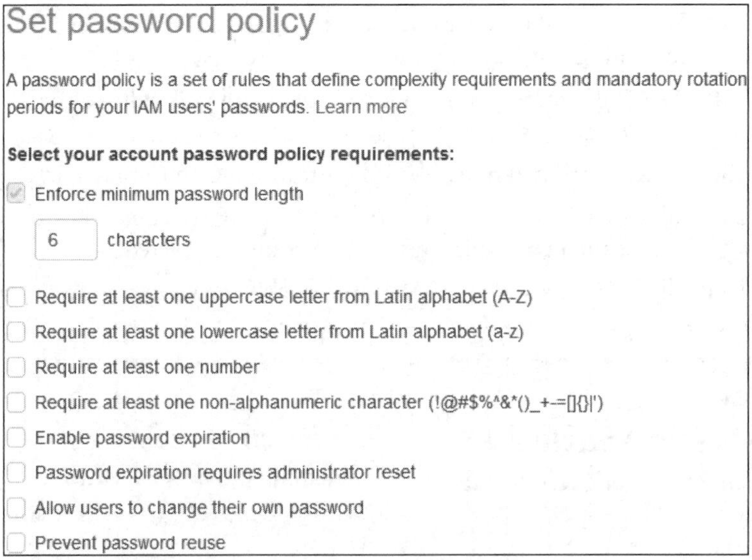

Figure 3-2   The options available for setting an IAM password policy

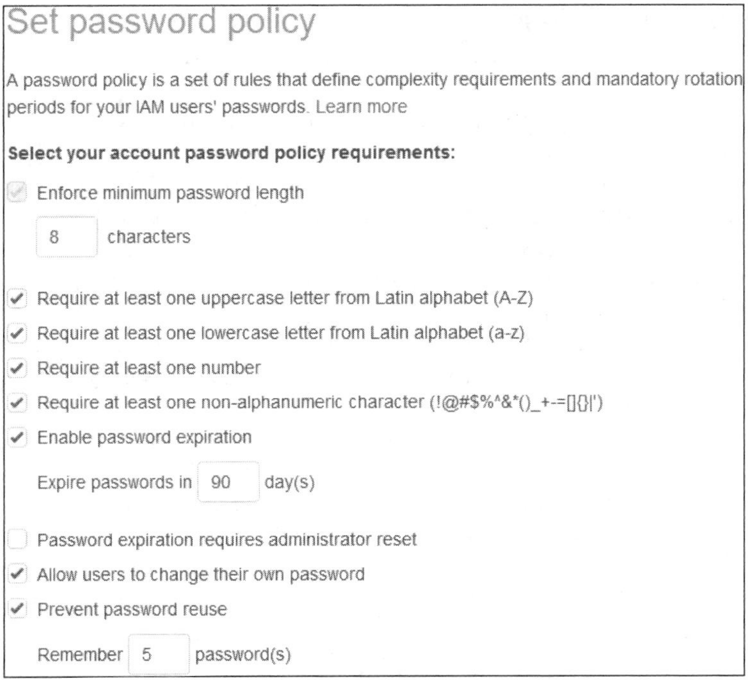

Set password policy

A password policy is a set of rules that define complexity requirements and mandatory rotation periods for your IAM users' passwords. Learn more

Select your account password policy requirements:

☑ Enforce minimum password length

    [8] characters

☑ Require at least one uppercase letter from Latin alphabet (A-Z)
☑ Require at least one lowercase letter from Latin alphabet (a-z)
☑ Require at least one number
☑ Require at least one non-alphanumeric character (!@#$%^&*()_+-=[]{}|')
☑ Enable password expiration

    Expire passwords in [90] day(s)

☐ Password expiration requires administrator reset
☑ Allow users to change their own password
☑ Prevent password reuse

    Remember [5] password(s)

Figure 3-3   Password policy options selected for the exercise

6. For the purposes of this exercise, we will set up a password policy with the following options selected:

   - Enforce minimum password length—change from the default 6 to 8
   - Require at least one uppercase letter
   - Require at least one lowercase letter
   - Require at least one number
   - Require at least one non-alphanumeric character
   - Enable password expiration—leave at the default 90 days
   - Allow users to change their own password
   - Prevent password reuse—leave at the default 5 passwords
   - Verify you have the options properly selected to match what is shown in Figure 3-3.

7. Click Save Changes.

8. Click on the Dashboard link on the left menu, and you will now see on your Security Status table that you have successfully enabled a password policy for IAM users.

IAM User Groups and Roles

Before we create an IAM user, it is important to understand what groups and roles are within AWS.

Groups are used to assign a standard set of permissions to users as they are added to the system. As you add more users, going through each user and assigning permissions can become a very labor-intensive process, and one that is often fraught with error. With the wide variety of services and permissions that AWS has across the various product offerings, you could easily end up with permissions profiles that have a few dozen different roles attached to them for some users, or lots of different groups based on each product and the level of access granted to it. Groups represent the way to create packages of settings that are maintained in a single location. As users are added to the system, they can be added to the appropriate groups and will automatically inherit the appropriate permissions in a consistent manner.

Roles in AWS are the granular permissions that users can be granted. Within each AWS service, there are multiple roles that allow different activities, such as reading data, creating data, deploying services, provisioning access, etc. These roles are then used to attach to users, or as mentioned previously, to groups that users are then assigned to. AWS has a large number of roles that are predefined that you can navigate through when you create groups based on your particular needs, and you can always modify their association with users or groups at any time.

 EXAM TIP The AWS system has predefined roles for every service offering that you can select to attach to groups. Keep in mind that within each service offering, there are several different roles that grant different types of access, such as read versus update, as well as a role that will allow full control over that particular service.

Exercise 3-3: Create an IAM User Account

1. If you are not already there, log into the IAM console at https://console.aws.amazon.com/iam.

2. When you log in this time with your root account, you will have to use the MFA that you previously set up, along with your root account password.

3. On the Security Status menu, click on Create Individual IAM Users and then click on Manage Users.

4. Click on the blue Add User button at the top of the page.

5. You will now be presented with the Add User wizard.

   a. For this exercise, you can pick any username you would like. For illustrative purposes, we will use "testuser."

   b. Under Account Access, check both boxes to enable AWS Console access and Programmatic access.

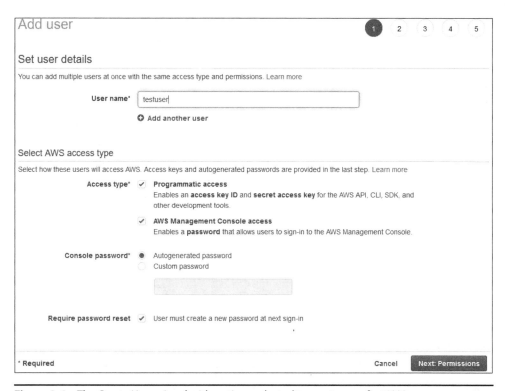

Figure 3-4   The Create User wizard with options selected to create your first IAM user

   c. Leave the default options selected to create an autogenerated password and to require the user to change their password at next sign-in. This will require them to select a password based on the policy you previously established.

   d. Your screen should now look like what is shown in Figure 3-4.

   e. Click on the Next: Permissions button.

6. You will now be at Set Permissions screen.

   a. Click on the Create Group button, as your account does not have any groups defined yet.

   b. On the Create Group menu, input a Group Name of **Admins**.

   c. Click on the top policy for Administrator Access.

   d. Click Create Group.

7. You will now have the new Admins group selected for the IAM user.

8. Click Next: Tags at the bottom.

9. The tags are optional, so we will not add any at this point. Click on the Next: Review button.

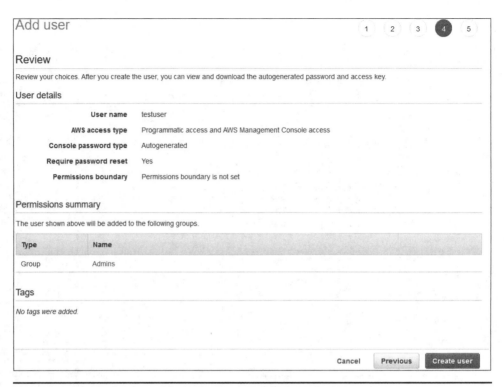

Figure 3-5 The final review of the IAM user creation before submission

10. You will now see a review of the user you are creating. Your screen should match what is shown in Figure 3-5.

11. Click Create User to finish the creation process.

12. On the confirmation page, you have the options to e-mail log-in instructions to someone to use the new account, as well as the ability to show the password and secret access key.

13. Click Close.

14. Click on the Dashboard link on the left menu.

15. You will now see in the Security Status display that all five activities have been completed.

Federated Access

A powerful way for providing user access to AWS is through federated access. With federated access, you can use technologies such as SAML or Microsoft Active Directory to provision users, rather than creating them manually through the IAM account process in the Console. The big advantage with using federated access is that users will use accounts and credentials they already have established to access AWS. This enables an organization to use already existing security and account practices, without having to worry about maintaining them in another system, as well as keeping all the user management and provisioning practices they already have. This also includes when a user is terminated access to an organization having that same termination immediately affect AWS access as well.

The most commonly used method for federated access today is through the SAML 2.0 standard.

SAML

SAML 2.0 is the latest standard put out by the nonprofit OASIS consortium and their Security Services Technical Committee and can be found at https://www.oasis-open.org/standards#samlv2.0. SAML is XML based, and it is used to exchange information used in the authentication and authorization processes between different parties. Specifically, it is used for information exchange between identity providers and service providers, and it contains within the XML block the required information that each system needs or provides. The 2.0 standard was adopted in 2005 and provides a standard framework for the XML assertions and standardized naming conventions for its various elements. In a federated system, when an entity authenticates through an identity provider, it sends a SAML assertion to the service provider containing all the information that the service provider requires to determine the identity, level of access warranted, or any other information or attributes about the entity.

User Reporting

As with any system that has a number of users on it, you will want a way to keep track of what users you have, what access they have, when they last logged in, and their status of being issued keys and when they were last rotated. This report is offered as a CSV download that you can either review directly from the CSV or import into any data or reporting tool you desire.

The report can be accessed from the left menu with the Credential Report button. You then only need to click on Download Report to have the report generated and available for downloading for whatever purposes you need. After you click to download the report, it will take a few moments to run, but will then present you with the download option that your browser uses.

AWS Support

Before we get into the specifics of security support, we need to discuss the overall support model and options that are available with AWS. When we created an account in our first exercise, we selected the free support option. However, while the free support is terrific for testing out various components to suit our purposes or for a user just starting to explore what AWS has to offer and evaluating features, it is not ideal for organizations that are more heavily invested in AWS, and certainly not for anyone running production business services in AWS.

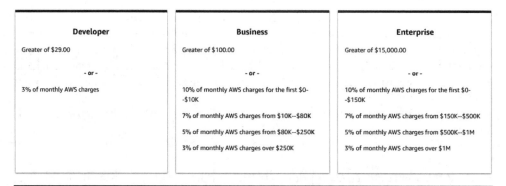

Figure 3-6 Overview of the developer, business, and enterprise support plan costs in AWS

Support Plan Options

AWS offers three different support plans beyond the free basic plan. These plans are

- **Developer**   Ideal for testing and early stages of development in AWS and needing support during business hours
- **Business**   Used for those with production workloads in AWS and desiring 24/7 support access
- **Enterprise**   Highest level of support and geared towards full optimization of your AWS experience and success

Of course, with any service in the cloud, the more resources you desire, the higher the costs will be, as shown in Figure 3-6.

Developer Support Plan

The developer support plan is ideal for those starting their early testing of AWS or development within AWS and want access to general guidance and technical support.

Highlights of developer support:

- **AWS Trusted Advisor**   Provides access to the seven core Advisor checks. This will give guidance on best practices of reducing costs, how to get the most out of performance, how to implement and improve fault tolerance, and how to improve security.
- **AWS Personal Health Dashboard**   Provides a view of overall AWS services and their current health status, along with the impact of any issues on your specific resources. This also includes API access to allow you to integrate with any monitoring and management systems you already have in place or want to use.

- **Technical support**   The developer support option provides access to cloud support engineers during normal business hours. It allows one contact on your account to open as many support cases as you need but does not allow all of your IAM accounts to access support. You must utilize the main delegated account to open support incidents. Support response times for the developer option are

  - Less than 24 hours for general guidance

  - Less than 12 hours for system problems and issues

- **Architecture Support**   Provides general guidance on AWS services and how they can be optimized for various use cases, expected workloads, or particular application requirements.

 EXAM TIP   The developer support plan only offers support during business hours. Remember that if production systems are being run and support is needed on a 24/7 basis, you will need to select either the business or enterprise support plans.

Business Support Plan

The business support plan is geared towards those with production workloads hosted in AWS and desiring 24/7 support. It also offers architectural guidance that is geared specifically to your systems and applications, as opposed to developer support that only offers general guidance.

- **AWS Trusted Advisor**   Unlike the developer support plan that only gives access to 7 Trusted Advisor checks, the business support plan gives access to the entire 115 checks that AWS offers, covering cost optimization, security, fault tolerance, performance, and service limits. Each check comes with recommendations based on best practices.

- **AWS Personal Health Dashboard**   The business support plan offers a personalized view of AWS services that you are using, along with alerts about any potential impacts.

- **Technical Support**   The business support plan offers 24/7 access to support engineers via phone, chat, or e-mail. Unlike the developer support plan that restricts access to just one account to open support incidents, the business support plan allows an unlimited number of contacts to open tickets. Support response times with the business support plan are

  - Less than 24 hours for general guidance

  - Less than 12 hours for system problems and issues

  - Less than 4 hours for production system problems

  - Less than 1 hour for production system outages

- **Architecture Support** Specific guidance geared towards AWS services and how they fit your particular needs, workloads, or application configurations.

- **AWS Support API** Customers have access to programmatic APIs for the AWS support center, enabling them to open, update, or close support tickets, as well as to manage Trust Advisor requests and statuses.

- **Third-Party Software Support** Guidance and configuration assistance with AWS interoperability with commonly used applications, operations systems, and platforms.

- **Access to Proactive Support Programs** With the business support plan, you have the option to purchase, for an additional fee, access to the infrastructure event management services. This provides architecture and scaling guidance in real time for support during the preparation and rollout of planed events, releases, or migrations.

Enterprise Support Plan

The enterprise support plan is geared towards offering a highly personal and responsive service to AWS customers at the highest levels. It builds on the business support plan and adds some more features:

- **Technical Support** The enterprise support plan offers 24/7 access to support engineers via phone, chat, or e-mail. The enterprise support plan allows an unlimited number of contacts to open tickets. Support response times with the business support plan are

  - Less than 24 hours for general guidance

  - Less than 12 hours for system problems and issues

  - Less than 4 hours for production system problems

  - Less than 1 hour for production system outages

  - Less than 15 minutes for critical system outages

- **Proactive Support Programs** With the enterprise support plan, you have access to specific reviews of your services and implementations in the areas of architecture, operations, and infrastructure event management.

- **Support Concierge** The concierge team is dedicated to working with enterprise support customers and are experts in billing and account issues, allowing you to quickly resolve any issues and alleviate focusing on account issues.

- **Account Onboarding** You are provided an AWS Technical Account Manager (TAM) to work with you on all issues and outages, as well as your access to AWS resources. The TAM will participate in disaster recovery planning and drills, as well as provide a personal and direct contact for any support or account issues.

Other Support Resources

Apart from the official support plans offered by AWS, a variety of resources are available that are more self-learning or community-support in nature.

AWS Professional Services

The AWS Professional Services group is another avenue for support and guidance on AWS services. The Professional Services group operates mostly based on a series of "offerings," which are a set of activities, documentation, and best practices that form a methodology for customers moving to the cloud. They are designed as a blueprint to quickly achieve outcomes and allow customers to finish projects and offer high reliability of outcomes.

The Professional Services group publishes the AWS Cloud Adoption Framework, which is focused on helping organizations with successful cloud adoption. The framework is geared towards helping an organization develop a comprehensive approach to cloud adoption and increasing the rate of adoption while also lowering the risk involved through the use of best practices.

Another key offering from the Professional Services group is working with the AWS Partner Network. The AWS Partner Network works complementary with the Professional Services group to offer consulting services and software to help with cloud adoption and achieving optimal results.

The Professional Services group offers a series of whitepapers and tech-talk webinars on various AWS services and offerings focused on best practices and cloud migrations. These are freely available. More information about AWS Professional Services can be found at https://aws.amazon.com/professional-services/.

Documentation

AWS maintains a vast library of freely available and accessible documentation online. This documentation covers pretty much any topic and service you would ever think of and tends to be well maintained and curated. You can access the AWS Documentation library at https://docs.aws.amazon.com/.

On the main page you will find "Guides and API References" for every AWS service offering. Clicking on any of the names will take you to the main page for that service. Most service pages are organized with the same main headings. This will differ some based on the type of service and which ones apply to it:

- A user guide (sometimes split out for different platforms, if applicable, such as Linux and Windows)
- An API reference
- A link to the pertinent section for that service in the AWS CLI Reference
- A developer guide

Apart from the documentation for specific service offerings, there are also major sections that are thematic and cross between service offerings, such as security, management, billing, and general reference documents.

Below the guides and API references is an extensive library of "Tutorials and Projects." This section contains how-to guides for many operations within AWS. Also included are reference links to many of the various SDKs and toolkits that are commonly used, including the AWS Command Line Interface.

Knowledge Center

The AWS Knowledge Center can be found at https://aws.amazon.com/premiumsupport/knowledge-center/.

The structure of the Knowledge Center is that of a typical FAQ page, organized by AWS services. Unlike your typical FAQ, however, the Knowledge Center has an enormous number of pages that are framed in a question-and-answer format. It is designed to work alongside and complement other AWS resources, such as documentation, discussion forums, and the AWS Support Center.

 EXAM TIP The Knowledge Center is an excellent way to learn about many different features of AWS and the types of questions and common issues customers face. Just going through a service you are starting to explore or already using and looking at the questions and answers can give a lot of insight into that service and give a good basis of the types of issues to be cognizant of in your own usage.

Discussion Forums

AWS hosts a discussion forum site to enable customers to help each other with specific problems and best practices guidance. It can be found at https://forums.aws.amazon.com/.

The forums are split into numerous categories to help organize information and serve as a starting point for navigation. There is also a search feature to help find information. The organizational structure of the forums is

- **Amazon Web Services**   Contains forums that are organized by AWS service offerings
- **AWS Startups**   Focused on users that are new to AWS and applicable assistance
- **AWS Web Site & Resources**   Offers forums for General Feedback, Quick Start Deployments, and specific forums based on development platforms and technologies, such as programming languages, the AWS Command Line Interface, and datasets.
- **Foreign Language Forums**   AWS offers forums for Japanese, German, Portuguese, Korean, and Indonesian customers.

Trusted Advisor

The AWS Trusted Advisor provides a dashboard to check whether your account configurations comply with established best practices. The Trusted Advisor is split into five areas of focus:

- **Cost Optimization**   Flags any resources that you have allocated and are incurring billing charges and are either not being used at the level they are allocated for or are allocated but inactive. This enables users to eliminate resources that are incurring billing charges and wasting money.
- **Performance**   Flags any configurations that are implemented in a way that might be preventing resources from reaching their full potential and limiting performance.
- **Security**   Flags any deficiencies in security configurations that do not meet established best practices
- **Fault Tolerance**   Flags any resources that are allocated but are configured in a way that makes them vulnerable to service interruptions, such as single points of failure with nonreplicated systems, or any systems that are not being backed up.
- **Service Limits**   Flags any services that you are using that are approaching their limits within AWS, such as number of instances of data objects or regional limitations.

Security Support Offerings

AWS provides dedicated support resources for all of their service offerings, and of course also provides specific guidance for security of data and systems, as it is a primary focus of AWS. The specific security support page can be found at https://aws.amazon.com/security/security-resources/.

On this security-focused page, you will find links to specific security resources within documentation, whitepapers, and best practice reference materials. You will also find links to the AWS Security Control Domains and security training resources. AWS does provide security information and documentation in over 20 languages to ensure compliance with regulations and systems throughout the world.

Chapter Review

In this chapter we covered the overall security concepts that apply to cloud environments and the various ways in which AWS implements them. We reviewed how to add users through IAM and how to enact security policies to protect your account and meet any organizational or regulatory requirements and policies. We then learned about the different support plans that are available to AWS users and the diverse resources for security support, including AWS Professional Services, documentation, the Knowledge Center, and discussion forums.

Questions

1. Which protocol is most commonly used for federated authentication systems?
   A. JSON
   B. SAML
   C. XML
   D. Node.js

2. Which security technology involves taking data of an arbitrary size or length and converting it to a fixed size?
   A. Hashing
   B. Tokenization
   C. Encryption
   D. Obfuscation

3. Which AWS support plan is best suited for those exploring AWS services and beginning to test deployments?
   A. Basic
   B. Business
   C. Developer
   D. Enterprise

4. Which AWS support service gives a report on configuration compliance with best practices?
   A. Knowledge Center
   B. IAM dashboard
   C. Professional Services
   D. Trusted Advisor

5. What type of encryption mechanism is used for data that is hosted and stored on a system?
   A. Data at rest
   B. Data in use
   C. Object
   D. Managed

6. What term refers to capabilities that are attached to an account and enable them to perform specific functions or control services?

   A. Groups

   B. Categories

   C. Roles

   D. Permissions

7. Which area of responsibility lies with the customer in a PaaS implementation?

   A. Application code

   B. Security

   C. Operating system

   D. Storage

8. Which AWS support plan offers response times of less than 15 minutes for critical system outages?

   A. Basic

   B. Enterprise

   C. Business

   D. Developer

9. Underutilized systems will be flagged under which component of the Trusted Advisor?

   A. Cost optimization

   B. Performance

   C. Fault tolerance

   D. Utilization

10. What should also be configured to improve the security of the root user for your account?

    A. Secondary password

    B. Recovery e-mail

    C. Encryption

    D. MFA

Questions and Answers

1. Which protocol is most commonly used for federated authentication systems?

   A. JSON

   B. SAML

   C. XML

   D. Node.js

   ☑ **B.** The Security Assertion Markup Language (SAML) is an open standard to facilitate the exchange of authentication and authorization data between two parties and is very commonly used with federated and web-based single sign-on (SSO) systems.

2. Which security technology involves taking data of an arbitrary size or length and converting it to a fixed size?

   A. Hashing

   B. Tokenization

   C. Encryption

   D. Obfuscation

   ☑ **A.** Hashing involves taking data of an arbitrary type, length, or size and using a function to map a value that is of a fixed size. Hashing can be applied to virtually any type of data object, including text strings, documents, images, binary data, and even virtual machine images.

3. Which AWS support plan is best suited for those exploring AWS services and beginning to test deployments?

   A. Basic

   B. Business

   C. Developer

   D. Enterprise

   ☑ **C.** The developer support plan is ideal for those starting their early testing of AWS or development within AWS and want access to general guidance and technical support.

4. Which AWS support service gives a report on configuration compliance with best practices?

   A. Knowledge Center

   B. IAM dashboard

   C. Professional Services

   D. Trusted Advisor

☑ **D.** The AWS Trusted Advisor provides a dashboard to check whether your account configurations comply with established best practices.

5. What type of encryption mechanism is used for data that is hosted and stored on a system?

  A. Data at rest

  B. Data in use

  C. Object

  D. Managed

☑ **A.** Data at rest refers to information stored on a system or device (versus data that is actively being transmitted across a network or between systems). The data can be stored in many different forms to fit within this category. Some examples include databases, file sets, spreadsheets, documents, tapes, archives, and even mobile devices.

6. What term refers to capabilities that are attached to an account and enable them to perform specific functions or control services?

  A. Groups

  B. Categories

  C. Roles

  D. Permissions

☑ **C.** Roles in AWS are the granular permissions that users can be granted. Within each AWS service, there are multiple roles that allow different activities, such as reading data, creating data, deploying services, provisioning access, etc.

7. Which area of responsibility lies with the customer in a PaaS implementation?

  A. Application code

  B. Security

  C. Operating system

  D. Storage

☑ **A.** The application code is the responsibility of the customer within a PaaS service model.

8. Which AWS support plan offers response times of less than 15 minutes for critical system outages?

  A. Basic

  B. Enterprise

  C. Business

  D. Developer

☑ **B.** The enterprise support plan offers response times of less than 15 minutes for critical system outages.

9. Underutilized systems will be flagged under which component of the Trusted Advisor?

   A. Cost optimization

   B. Performance

   C. Fault tolerance

   D. Utilization

   ☑ **A.** The cost optimization component of the Trusted Advisor will flag any resources that are incurring billing charges but are either inactive or underutilized.

10. What should also be configured to improve the security of the root user for your account?

    A. Secondary password

    B. Recovery e-mail

    C. Encryption

    D. MFA

    ☑ **D.** Multifactor authentication (MFA) should always be configured on the root account of your AWS account to improve security and mitigate any potential access or damage that could occur if the password were ever disclosed or compromised.

Technology

In this chapter, you will learn the following Domain 3 topics:
- Define methods of deploying and operating in the AWS Cloud
- Define the AWS global infrastructure
- Identify the core AWS services
- Identity resources for technology support

Domain 3 covers the technical aspects of the AWS Cloud. This includes the tools and utilities to get users up and running in AWS, as well as code development. The core AWS services are highlighted, along with their key features and how they can improve upon legacy systems and hosting that most companies already use. Many support options are available for AWS technical aspects, including support plans, documentation, and user forums.

Deploying and Operating in the AWS Cloud

AWS offers a large suite of utilities and developer tools to enable quick migration into AWS and the ability to develop and support applications fully within the AWS environment. These tools are built upon popular standards and programming languages, are fully managed by AWS, and will scale to the needs of any developers, without the need to provision additional resources.

AWS Management Console

The AWS Management Console is the main resource where you can control all of your AWS services and perform any operations against them.

To access the AWS Management Console you can go to https://console.aws.amazon.com and log in with your root credentials. When you log in, you will be presented with the AWS Management Console dashboard, as shown in Figure 4-1.

Across the top of the Management Console are dropdown menus to gain access to most AWS services and resources. Clicking on the Services button will display a menu listing all AWS services with clickable names to get to each service's dashboard, as shown in Figure 4-2.

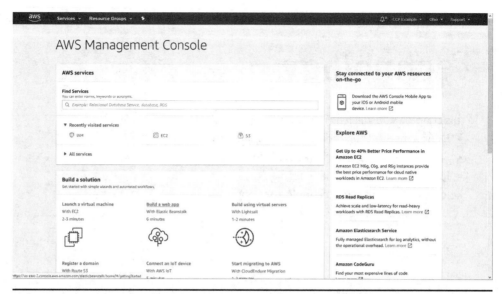

Figure 4-1 The AWS Management Console dashboard

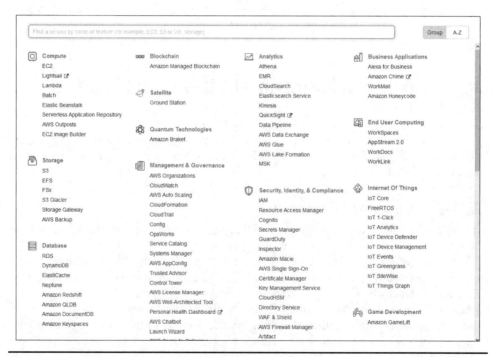

Figure 4-2 The Services menu in the AWS Management Console provides clickable access to the dashboard for all AWS services.

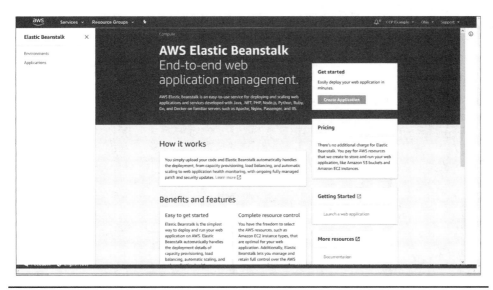

Figure 4-3 The dashboard for the Elastic Beanstalk service. The Create Application button on the right starts the process of launching a new application.

For example, with the Services menu expanded, clicking on Elastic Beanstalk takes you to the dashboard for that service, where you can access any applications you already have provisioned, or create a new application using the Create Application button on the right side of the screen, as shown in Figure 4-3.

On any screen, in the upper-right corner of the console is a dropdown menu to change regions that you are viewing. As shown in Figure 4-4, each region is listed and is clickable. For some services that are global in nature, you will not see regions displayed within the dashboard for that service.

 EXAM TIP As you are learning about the AWS Core services, keep track of which ones are global in nature and not bound to regions. Many services are offered at a global level, and no selection or configuration in regard to regions or availability zones is necessary.

From any screen you can also directly access the support and documentation for AWS services by clicking on the Support dropdown in the upper-right corner, as shown in Figure 4-5.

AWS CLI

The AWS Command Line Interface (CLI) provides a way to manage AWS services and perform many administrative functions without having to use the web-based Management Console. Through the use of CLI, users can also script and automate many functions through whatever programming languages they are familiar with or desire to use for automation. Each AWS service has CLI commands that are pertinent to it and can be found in the AWS documentation.

Figure 4-4
The Regions dropdown menu, allowing you to switch regions from Console dashboards

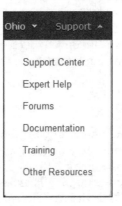

US East (N. Virginia)	us-east-1
US East (Ohio)	us-east-2
US West (N. California)	us-west-1
US West (Oregon)	us-west-2
Africa (Cape Town)	af-south-1
Asia Pacific (Hong Kong)	ap-east-1
Asia Pacific (Mumbai)	ap-south-1
Asia Pacific (Seoul)	ap-northeast-2
Asia Pacific (Singapore)	ap-southeast-1
Asia Pacific (Sydney)	ap-southeast-2
Asia Pacific (Tokyo)	ap-northeast-1
Canada (Central)	ca-central-1
Europe (Frankfurt)	eu-central-1
Europe (Ireland)	eu-west-1
Europe (London)	eu-west-2
Europe (Milan)	eu-south-1
Europe (Paris)	eu-west-3
Europe (Stockholm)	eu-north-1
Middle East (Bahrain)	me-south-1
South America (São Paulo)	sa-east-1

Figure 4-5
The Support menu allows direct access to AWS support options and documentation.

Ohio ▾   Support ▴

Support Center

Expert Help

Forums

Documentation

Training

Other Resources

The AWS CLI is available for Windows, macOS, and Linux and requires a small software installation to add the AWS capabilities to their command line tools. You will also need to have outbound access on port 443 allowed through your network and firewalls. The AWS CLI also requires the use of an access/secret key for a user that can be obtained from the IAM portal.

Information on how to set up and use the AWS CLI can be found at https://docs.aws .amazon.com/cli.

AWS Developer Tools

AWS provides a suite of developer tools and services that are fully managed and will assist with code building, committing to repositories, and deployment to systems when ready for testing and release.

AWS Developer Tools and SDKs

AWS offers a variety of Software Development Kits (SDKs) that will facilitate developers across the most popular programming languages. SDKs are also offered specific to mobile and Internet of Things (IoT) development.

SDKs are offered for the following programming languages:

- JavaScript
- Python
- PHP
- .NET
- Ruby
- Java
- Go
- Node.js
- C++

Mobile SDKs are offered for the following platforms:

- iOS
- Android
- React Native
- Mobile Web
- Unity
- Xamarin

For a complete list of SDKs available, please see https://aws.amazon.com/getting-started/tools-sdks.

NOTE You are always free to use any SDKs you are familiar with or your development teams already have processes in place with. Many of these are officially supported by AWS and integrated into their infrastructure, but this is not exclusive. Keep in mind the use of other SDKs may not have the full feature set as those officially supported by AWS.

CodeBuild

AWS CodeBuild is a fully featured code building service that will compile and test code, as well as build deployment packages that are ready for implementation. CodeBuild is a fully managed AWS service that will automatically scale to the needs of developers, alleviating their need to manage and scale a system. With the ability to auto-scale, developers will not have to wait for queues for code building or testing. AWS offers a variety of prebuilt environments, or you can customize your own for specific unique needs.

CodeCommit

AWS CodeCommit is an AWS managed service for secure Git repositories. With the popularity of Git for code versioning, the AWS service allows users to be up and running quickly and in a secure environment, without having to configure and manage their own repository systems. AWS CodeCommit will automatically scale to the needs of users and is completely compatible with any tools and software that have Git capabilities.

CodeDeploy

AWS CodeDeploy is a managed deployment service that can deploy code fully across AWS services or on-premises servers. The service is designed to handle complex deployments and ensure that all pieces and configurations are properly deployed, allowing a savings in time spent on verification after rollouts. CodeDeploy will fully scale to any resources that are needed.

Configuration Management

With many AWS customers using large numbers of instances and services within AWS, the need for configuration management tools to keep systems uniform and consistent is very important. AWS offers a variety of tools to implement and audit configurations across services.

Systems Manager

The AWS Systems Manager allows you consolidate data from AWS services and automate tasks across all of your services. It allows for a holistic view of all of your AWS services, while also allowing you to create logical groups of resources that can then be viewed in a consolidated manner. Within Systems Manager there are many components that allow you to perform different administrative tasks.

- **OpsCenter** Provides a consolidated view for developers and operations staff to view and investigate any operational issues. Data from many different resources, such as CloudTrail logs, CloudWatch alarms, metrics, information about AWS configuration changes, and event and account information are all centralized.

It allows for a quick view of your entire environment and helps diagnose problems as quickly as possible.

- **Explorer** A customizable dashboard that provides information on the health of your entire AWS environment and can consolidate data spanning multiple accounts and regions.

- **AWS AppConfig** Provides an API and console method for applying configuration changes across AWS services from a centralized service. This is done in much the same way code is deployed out to multiple locations. AppConfig can quickly deploy configuration changes to different instances of compute services and ensure they are applied in a uniform and consistent manner.

- **Resource groups** Allows for the logical grouping of resources within AWS for how they are presented within the Systems Manager. This allows a user to group services by application, department, tier, or any other manner they find useful, rather than looking at all resources collectively.

 EXAM TIP Keep in mind the concept of resource groups, especially with large deployments within AWS. The use of resource groups can help segment services to specific applications and groups and assist with monitoring your services within AWS.

- **Insights dashboard** The automatically created visual dashboard of operational data from throughout your AWS account. As service data is consolidated, the dashboard is automatically populated and organized with common views into CloudTrail data, configurations, inventory, and compliance.

- **Inventory** Collects information from all services you have provisioned within AWS, including configuration and licensing information. It enables a central location to view and track all assets.

- **Automation** Provides a setup of predefined playbooks to do common repetitive tasks, but also allows for users to create their own playbooks that are appropriate for their specific services.

- **Run command** Provides a way to run commands on servers within AWS without having to actually access them via SSH or PowerShell. The Run command logs all activities under CloudTrail and allows for granular access control via IAM.

- **Systems Manager** Allows for accessing Shell and CLI for managing EC2 instances via a browser and without needing to use keys or expose ports from systems. All activities are fully auditable via CloudWatch and CloudTrail.

- **Patch Manager** Allows for automatically handling patching of systems across EC2 or on-premises systems through the use of baselines. Patch Manager allows for the scheduling of patching and auditing the status of them.

- **Maintenance Window** Enables the execution of administrative and maintenance tasks during specific time windows that are best suited for the specific service and its user base.

- **Distributor**   Allows for the central storage, distribution, and installation of software packages to instances within AWS, including software agents. You can use Distributor to push out software files and then use the Run command to automate installation and configuration of them.
- **State Manager**   Handles configuration management tasks across EC2 or on-premises systems. It can automatically apply configuration changes to systems on a schedule that you choose and provide compliance overviews that they have been correctly and uniformly applied.
- **Parameter Store**   Provides a way to store configuration data for your applications. This can be either plain-text strings or passwords used to access services such as databases. A main benefit of the Parameter Store is the ability to use the same key but contain different values for systems. For example, you could have a hostname for a database or API call that gets a different value for systems that are flagged as development, test, or production but allows your code to remain the same throughout.

OpsWorks
AWS OpsWorks provides managed instances of Puppet and Chef. Both are well known and widely used automation and server configuration tools used throughout the IT world. The AWS implementation can be used for configuration automation for EC2 instances within AWS, as well as on-premises instances. Within OpsWorks, AWS offers the AWS OpsWorks for Chef Automate, AWS OpsWorks for Puppet Enterprise, and AWS OpsWorks Stacks, which allows you to manage systems within EC2 as stacks and layers, each with their own independent configurations with Chef.

AWS Global Infrastructure

AWS runs a very large cloud infrastructure that is distributed throughout the world. This network is divided into different segments that are geographically based, such as regions and availability zones. AWS also runs a network of Edge services throughout the world that serve a portion of AWS services and are optimized for low-latency and responsiveness to requests.

AWS Regions

AWS organizes resources throughout the world in regions. Each region is a group of logical data centers, called Availability Zones. While each region may seem like it is a data center or a physical location, it is actually a collection of independent data centers that are grouped and clustered together, providing redundancy and fault tolerance.

When you provision resources within AWS, they can exist in only one region and are hosted on the physical hardware present at it. That does not mean you cannot replicate instances and virtual machines across multiple regions and around the world, but each individual instance only exists in one region. However, some resources within AWS are global in nature and not bound to specific regions, such as the IAM services and the CloudFront service. Both of those regions will show up as "global" instead of a specific region.

You can see the list of current AWS regions in Table 4-1. The current list can always be found at https://docs.aws.amazon.com/AWSEC2/latest/UserGuide/using-regions-availability-zones.html.

 EXAM TIP Not all AWS regions are available to all AWS accounts. For example, the us-gov-west-1 is restricted to U.S. federal government accounts, and AWS accounts from China are restricted to special Beijing and Ningxia regions that are not otherwise accessible.

Code	Name
us-east-2	United States East (Ohio)
us-east-1	United States East (Northern Virginia)
us-west-1	United States West (Northern California)
us-west-2	United States West (Oregon)
af-south-1	Africa (Cape Town)
ap-east-1	Asia Pacific (Hong Kong)
ap-south-1	Asia Pacific (Mumbai)
ap-northeast-3	Asia Pacific (Osaka-Local)
ap-northeast-2	Asia Pacific (Seoul)
ap-southeast-1	Asia Pacific (Singapore)
ap-southeast-2	Asia Pacific (Sydney)
ap-northeast-1	Asia Pacific (Tokyo)
ca-central-1	Canada (Central)
eu-central-1	Europe (Frankfurt)
eu-west-1	Europe (Ireland)
eu-west-2	Europe (London)
eu-south-1	Europe (Milan)
eu-west-3	Europe (Paris)
eu-north-1	Europe (Stockholm)
me-south-1	Middle East (Bahrain)
sa-east-1	South America (São Paulo)
us-gov-west-1	GovCloud (United States)

Table 4-1 AWS Global Regions

When you provision a resource, the decision of which region to locate it in can depend on a few different factors:

- **Customer locations**   It makes sense to host your applications and resources closest to your customers. This will yield the fastest network times and responsiveness. The more global your business is, the more important it will be to spread resources around, but for many smaller businesses, it is easy to locate everything close to your location.

- **Security requirements**   It may make sense, depending on your application's needs and your appetite for risk, to completely separate resources or instances. While this can certainly be done logically within any region, you can also take the step of using completely different regions.

- **Regulatory requirements**   Many jurisdictions have regulatory requirements that dictate how personal and financial data can be used and transported. In many instances they are required to stay within geographic areas or within their own borders. The many regions that AWS offers make compliance with jurisdictional requirements a lot easier for companies.

 EXAM TIP   The use of regions for regulatory compliance is very important. Most regulations are built upon where the data resides or is being processed, and the ability within AWS to control, with most services, where that happens makes compliance much easier!

Service Endpoints
To keep order and make it easier to know what service you are using, as well as the region hosting it, all AWS services use endpoints that are formulaic in nature. This enables anyone with knowledge of the AWS topography to quickly know where and what a service is just by seeing the endpoint.

The construction of AWS service endpoints uses the following formula:

AWS service designation + AWS region + amazonaws.com

An example endpoint is ec2.eu-west-2.amazonaws.com

This example would be for an EC2 instance located in the Europe West 2 region (London). All services follow this type of nomenclature, and you will see it used throughout the sections on specific services. You may have seen this naming convention already through services you have used as a customer or URLs that are provided for resources.

Availability Zones
While regions represent a group or cluster of physical data centers, an AWS Availability Zone represents those actual physical locations. Each AWS data center is built with fully independent and redundant power, cooling, networking, and physical computing hardware. All network connections are dedicated lines, supporting the highest possible throughput and lowest levels of latency.

As each region is made up of multiple Availability Zones, there are direct connections for networking access between them, and all traffic is encrypted. This allows resources within a region to be spread out and clustered between the Availability Zones, without worrying about latency or security. Replication between Availability Zones allows for high availability should one of them experience an incident, such as a power outage, earthquake, or other natural disaster. All Availability Zones within a region are separated physically but are still within 60 miles (100 kilometers) of each other.

When you provision resources within AWS, you will select the region from one of those listed in Table 4-1, but then you will also select the Availability Zone within that region. This will be designated by a letter after the region, such as eu-south-1a. The list will contain all of those that are available within that region, increasing letters through the alphabet. However, when you are presented with the list of Availability Zones, they will be in a randomized order to better facilitate distribution and prevent users from just selecting the first one listed and everything ending up on the "a" Availability Zone.

Edge Locations

To provide optimal responsiveness for customers, AWS maintains a network of Edge locations throughout the world to provide ultra-low-latency access to data. These locations are geographically dispersed throughout the world to be close to customers and organizations in order to provide the fastest response times. Unlike regular AWS regions and Availability Zones, Edge locations are optimized to perform a narrow set of tasks and duties, allowing them to be optimally tuned and maintained for their intended focus, without being burdened by the full range of AWS services. Figure 4-6 shows the current location of Edge services. The current map can always be found at https://aws.amazon .com/cloudfront/features/.

Figure 4-6   AWS Edge locations throughout the world

Services That Use Edge

As mentioned, Edge locations run a minimal set of services to optimize delivery speeds.

- **Amazon CloudFront** A content delivery network (CDN) that allows cached copies of data and content to be distributed on Edge servers closest to customers. This also allows repeated access to data without having to reach back to the source systems each time. Data transfers from AWS Services to CloudFront are free and do not count towards any bandwidth metering or caps.
- **Amazon Route 53** The AWS DNS service that provides very fast, robust, and redundant lookup services.
- **AWS Shield** The AWS Distributed Denial of Service (DDoS) protection service that constantly monitors and reacts to any DDoS attacks.
- **AWS WAF** The AWS Web Application Firewall (WAF) that monitors and protects against web exploits and attacks based on rules that inspect traffic and requests.
- **Lambda@Edge** Provides a runtime environment for application code to be run on a CDN without having to provision systems or manage them. Customers pay only for the compute time they use.

Core AWS Services

AWS offers a large number of core services that are widely used and well known throughout the IT world. While we will not go through all services offered by AWS, we will touch on the most prominent ones in each category:

- Administrative, monitoring, and security services
- Networking and content delivery
- Storage
- Compute services
- Databases
- Automation
- End user computing

Administrative, Monitoring, and Security Services

AWS offers robust monitoring and auditing tools that span the breadth of all AWS service offerings. Monitoring systems are designed to collect and consolidate event data and auditing information from any services allocated under your account and provide them to you from a uniform and centralized dashboard.

CloudWatch

CloudWatch is the AWS service for monitoring and measuring services running within the AWS environment. It provides data and insights on application performance and how it may change over time, resource utilization, and a centralized and consolidated view of the overall health of systems and services. It is very useful to developers, engineers, and managers.

With any IT system, large amounts of data are produced in the form of system and application logs, but also data on performance and metrics. Across large systems, this can result in a large amount of data that is coming from many different sources. This can pose considerable challenges ranging from anyone looking to synthesize the data and formulate a picture of system health and performance, down to developers looking for specific events or instances within applications. CloudWatch collects and consolidates all of this data into a single service, making it much easier and more efficient to access. With this consolidation, developers and managers can see a picture of their overall systems and how they are performing, versus looking at individual systems or components of systems separately.

CloudWatch also integrates with the full range of services that AWS offers. If you are using a combination of different services, rather than having a dashboard and data for each individual service, you can get a full picture of everything together. Cloud-Watch even has agents that can be used to monitor on-premises systems, along with those hosted in AWS, for those that are using a hybrid cloud model. All of the data that is collected by CloudWatch is published with detailed one-minute metrics, but also offers the availability of custom metrics that can be done with one-second granularity, offering developers the ability to really drill down to the data points that they need. CloudWatch will keep data for up to 15 months.

Apart from the consolidation and presentation of data, CloudWatch extends its powerful capabilities with the concept of alarms. Alarms are based on predefined thresholds or through the use of machine learning algorithms and can trigger automated processes as a result. A prime example of the use of alarms is for auto-scaling based upon load or other thresholds, both with increasing and decreasing of allocated resources. Alarms can also be used to trigger workflows across the different AWS services since they are done from a consolidated standpoint and are not siloed within a particular service.

CloudTrail

CloudTrail is the AWS service for performing auditing and compliance within your AWS account. CloudTrail pairs with CloudWatch to analyze all the logs and data collected from the services within your account, which can then be audited and monitored for all activities done by users and admins within your account. This enables a full compliance capability and will store an historical record of all account activities. Should any investigations become necessary, all of the data is preserved and easily searchable.

CloudTrail will log all account activities performed, regardless of the method through which they were done. It logs all activity through the Management Console, CLI, and any API calls that are made, along with the originating IP address and all time and date data.

If any unauthorized changes are made, or if a change causes a disruption in services or system problems, the logs and reports available can enable an admin to quickly determine what was done and by whom.

CloudTrail also has the ability to trigger automation processes based on detected events. For example, if a certain type of API call is made, CloudTrail can trigger certain alerts to happen, or even the initiation of policies or other service changes.

AWS Shield

AWS Shield provides protection from and mitigation of DDoS attacks on AWS services. It is always active and monitoring AWS services, providing continual coverage without needing to engage AWS support for assistance should an attack occur. AWS Shield comes in two different service categories: Standard and Advanced.

Standard coverage is provided at no additional charge and is designed to protect against common DDoS attacks, especially for any accounts utilizing CloudFront and Route 53. This will protect websites and applications from the most frequently occurring attacks and virtually all known attacks on Layer 3 and 4 against CloudFront and Route 53.

For accounts that use more complex and large systems across EC2, ELB, and many other services, there is an Advanced tier of service that comes at an additional cost. This advanced offering protects against a wider range of attacks and includes more sophisticated mitigation capabilities, along with 24-hour access to the AWS DDoS Response team. The Advanced tier will provide the best protection against attacks that can incur substantial costs from resource utilization.

AWS WAF

AWS WAF is a web application firewall that protects web applications against many common attacks. AWS WAF comes with an array of preconfigured rules from AWS that will offer comprehensive protection based on common top security risks, but you also have the ability to create your own rules. The AWS WAF includes an API that can be used to automate rule creation and deployment of them to your allocated resources. Also included is a real-time view into your web traffic that you can then use to automatically create new rules and alerts.

AWS WAF is included at no additional cost for anyone who has purchased the AWS Shield Advanced tier. If you are not utilizing the Advanced Shield tier, you can use AWS WAF separately and will only incur costs based on the number of rules you create and the number of requests they service.

 EXAM TIP Remember the difference between Shield and WAF. Shield operates at the Layer 3 and 4 network levels and is used to prevent DDoS attacks, versus WAF that operates at the Layer 7 content level and can take action based on the specific contents of web traffic and requests.

Networking and Content Delivery

AWS offers robust networking and content delivery systems that are designed to optimize low latency and responsiveness to any queries, as well as complete fault tolerance and high availability. On top of the base network offers are robust security offerings through a Virtual Private Cloud topography, that include multiple layers of security controls, load balancing, and DNS services.

Virtual Private Cloud

With Amazon Virtual Private Cloud (Amazon VPC), you can create a logically defined space within AWS to create an isolated virtual network. Within this network, you retain full control over how the network is defined and allocated. You fully control the IP space, subnets, routing tables, and network gateway settings within your VPC, and you have full use of both IPv4 and IPv6.

You can provision network topographies within VPC much like you would in any kind of data center. You can have both public-facing and private network segments. For example, you can have one network segment that is open to the Internet where you host applications like web systems and other network segments that are not exposed to the Internet where you can host databases and other protected systems.

A common use for VPC is for disaster recovery planning. An organization can replicate network configurations and topographies from other cloud systems or from their own on-premise data centers into AWS for a low cost. An organization can regularly import their virtual machine instances into AWS, while also having the ability to easily replicate them back to the origin once a disaster situation has been recovered from. This allows an organization to get up to full resource levels and only incur substantial costs when it is actually needed to sustain operations, rather than paying for full systems at all times, like typically would be required.

AWS VPC also has the ability for an organization to essentially extend their corporate network into the cloud. By connecting your corporate network to AWS VPC, all of your current security mechanisms, such as firewalls, are retained and the resources in AWS inherit the same protections as if they were within your corporate network. This enables the use of storage and virtual machines in AWS, while retaining your already existing resources. Rather than having to buy additional hardware, especially for projects that are temporary, you can leverage AWS resources and only pay for what is needed and when it is needed.

Security Groups   Security groups in AWS are virtual firewalls that are used to control inbound and outbound traffic. Security groups are applied on the actual instance within a VPC versus at the subnet level. This means that in a VPC where you have many services or virtual machines deployed, each one can have different security groups applied to them. In fact, each instance can have up to five security groups applied to it, allowing different policies to be enforced and maintain granularity and flexibility for administrators and developers.

When you launch an instance of a service like EC2, you specify a security group in the initial configuration, or it will automatically assign to the default group if you do not. You can also create a new security group on the fly when you launch an EC2 instance if necessary. Security groups that are created can only be used within the VPC specified when they were created. The following also apply to security groups:

- Security groups can have different rules for inbound and outbound traffic.
  - By default, security groups allow all outbound traffic, but no inbound rules are applied by default.

- When specifying rules, you do them in the format of things allowed, not things denied.
- Security groups will automatically allow traffic that is in response to a request made by an allowed rule. For example, if an inbound request is allowed to be made, the corresponding reply is allowed to be made as well, regardless of what the rules specifically allow.

ACLs   Access control lists (ACLs) are security layers on the VPC that control traffic at the subnet level. This differs from security groups that are on each specific instance. However, many times both will be used for additional layers of security. The following are key aspects of ACLs:

- A VPC comes with a default ACL that allows all inbound and outbound traffic.
- Any custom ACLs will by default deny all inbound and outbound traffic until specific rules are applied to them.
- Every subnet must have an ACL assigned to it, either the default ACL or a custom one.
  - Each subnet may only have one ACL attached to it, but ACLs can be used for multiple subnets.
- An ACL is composed of a numbered set of rules that are processed in order.
- ACLs can have different rules for both inbound and outbound traffic.
  - Differing from security groups, an ACL can have both allow and deny rules.
- Unlike security groups, ACL rules do not automatically have state and allow responses to queries. If an inbound request is made and allowed, an applicable outbound rule must be in place to allow the response to transmit.

Subnets   Within a VPC, you must define a block of IP addresses that are available to it. These are called a Classless Inter-Domain Routing (CIDR) block. By default a VPC will be created with a CIDR of 172.31.0.0/16. This default block will encompass all IP addresses from 172.31.0.0 to 172.31.255.255.

You can also choose to define your own CIDR block using the same notation as a traditional data center with block sizes between /16 and /28. The smaller the number, the larger the number of addresses that are available to it. While the default block starts with 172.31, you can also specify your own desired block of addresses such as 10.10 or 192.168. This is useful if you are migrating applications into AWS or using a VPC that will also include your local network and need to match up with specifications you are already using.

Subnets are very useful for segmenting your VPC. You can use subnets to split up types of systems, public vs. private systems, or to apply different security groups. For example, if you have an application that has public-facing web servers along with back-end application or database servers, you can place the two types of systems in separate subnets. That way, you can apply a security group to the public-facing servers to allow

Internet access and a different security group to the application/database servers to only allow connections from the web servers, not from the public Internet. You can use routing tables to connect subnets across the AWS infrastructure for your particular needs.

> **NOTE** While the default subnet configuration for AWS uses IPv4 addressing, IPv6 is also available if desired or required.

Elastic Load Balancing

Elastic Load Balancing is used to distribute traffic across the AWS infrastructure. This can be done on varying degrees of granularity, ranging from spanning across multiple Availability Zones or within a single Availability Zone. It is focused on fault tolerance by implementing high availability, security, and auto-scaling capabilities. There are three different types of load balancing under its umbrella: application load balancer, network load balancer, and classic load balancer.

Application load balancing is most typically related to web traffic on both HTTP and HTTPS protocols. It has the ability to analyze the actual contents of the traffic and make determinations for routing and balancing based on rules. It is a very powerful method of load balancing that allows developers to optimize the responsiveness of their applications and segment traffic for either security or performance reasons. Application load balancing operates at Layer 7 of the OSI model, which lends to the ability to scope load balancing rules that are very specific to each individual application and the underlying ways in which they are architected. Application load balancing within AWS operates within a VPC, so it can be used across hybrid cloud models as well.

> **NOTE** Layer 7 of the OSI model pertains to the actual web traffic and content. Developers can take advantage of data such as the HTTP method, URL, parameters, headers, etc., in order to tune load balancing based on the specifics of their applications and the type of traffic and user queries it receives.

Network load balancing is best where performance is key and there are potentially very high levels of traffic. Network load balancing is done at the Layer 4 level of the OSI model, so it is purely based on protocols and source/destination of traffic. It does not have the capabilities of application load balancing, where it can analyze the actual content of traffic and make decisions based on it. It also operates within a VPC, so it can bridge between different environments in a hybrid model and is capable of handling millions of requests per second while maintaining ultra-low latency. A network load balancer is an optimal service to use where sudden or volatile traffic patterns are anticipated with data access, as it can better handle such loads versus application load balancing.

The third and final type of load balancing is the classic load balancing service. This is only used for basic load balancing between EC2 instances that were building on the EC2-Classic network and is not used for modern applications and new services.

Route 53

Amazon Route 53 is a robust, scalable, and highly available DNS service. Rather than running their own DNS services or being dependent on another commercial service, an organization can utilize Route 53 to transform names into their IP address, as well as having full IPv6 compatibility and access. Route 53 can be used for services that reside inside AWS, as well as those outside of AWS.

Extending on traditional DNS services, Route 53 has the ability to configure health checks and monitor systems, enabling the routing of DNS queries to healthy systems or those with lower load. Traditional DNS systems will only rotate between IP addresses that are configured for a name and do not have the ability to make informed decisions on where to route based on the health of systems or the current look of traffic. For example, Route 53 DNS resolution can return different answers based on geographic location, current latency of systems, or pure round-robin. Route 53 is fully integrated with the full suite of AWS services and can automatically handle DNS assignments for any service, such as EC2, CloudFront, Elastic Beanstalk, etc.

Along with all the other AWS services, pricing for Route 53 is based upon what features you use and the number of queries you get.

CloudFront

Amazon CloudFront is a CDN that allows for delivery of data and media to users with the lowest levels of latency and the highest levels of transfer speeds. This is done by having CloudFront systems distributed across the entire AWS global infrastructure and fully integrated with many AWS services, such as S3, EC2, and Elastic Load Balancing. CloudFront optimizes speed and delivery by directing user queries to the closest locations to their requests. This is especially valuable and useful for high-resource-demand media such as live and streaming video.

CloudFront offers extensive security benefits to account holders that are included in the standard costs for the service. This includes the ability to create custom SSL certificates through the AWS Certificate Manager. CloudFront also includes built-in security protections from the AWS Shield Standard, which is also included at no additional cost.

CloudFront allows developers and administrators full access to configuration options through the standard array of AWS tools, including APIs and the Management Console.

Storage

AWS offers extremely fast and expandable storage to meet the needs of any application or system. These offerings range from block storage used by EC2 instances to the widely used object storage of S3. AWS offers different tiers of storage to meet specific needs of production data processing systems versus those for archiving and long-term storage.

Elastic Block Store

Amazon Elastic Block Storage (EBS) is high-performance block storage that is used in conjunction with EC2 where high-throughput data operations are required. This will typically include file systems, media services, and relational and nonrelational databases. There are four types of EBS volumes that a user can pick from to meet their specific needs.

Two of the volume types feature storage backed by solid-state drives (SSDs) and two use traditional hard disk drives (HDDs). Figure 4-7 shows the four types of EBS volumes and their key technical specifications.

NOTE   As with all AWS services, there is constant change and new types of volumes being introduced. In August 2020, AWS announced a new io2 EBS volume type that will double the input/output operations per second (IOPS) from io1 and increases the level of reliability. You can create new volumes with io2 type or can convert new volumes to it.

	Solid State Drives (SSD)		Hard Disk Drives (HDD)	
Volume Type	EBS Provisioned IOPS SSD (io1)	EBS General Purpose SSD (gp2)*	Throughput Optimized HDD (st1)	Cold HDD (sc1)
Short Description	Highest performance SSD volume designed for latency-sensitive transactional workloads	General Purpose SSD volume that balances price performance for a wide variety of transactional workloads	Low cost HDD volume designed for frequently accessed, throughput intensive workloads	Lowest cost HDD volume designed for less frequently accessed workloads
Use Cases	I/O-intensive NoSQL and relational databases	Boot volumes, low-latency interactive apps, dev & test	Big data, data warehouses, log processing	Colder data requiring fewer scans per day
API Name	io1	gp2	st1	sc1
Volume Size	4 GB - 16 TB	1 GB - 16 TB	500 GB - 16 TB	500 GB - 16 TB
Max IOPS**/Volume	64,000	16,000	500	250
Max Throughput***/Volume	1,000 MB/s	250 MB/s	500 MB/s	250 MB/s
Max IOPS/Instance	80,000	80,000	80,000	80,000
Max Throughput/Instance	2,375 MB/s	2,375 MB/s	2,375 MB/s	2,375 MB/s
Price	$0.125/GB-month $0.065/provisioned IOPS	$0.10/GB-month	$0.045/GB-month	$0.025/GB-month
Dominant Performance Attribute	IOPS	IOPS	MB/s	MB/s

Figure 4-7   The four types of EBS volumes along with the key technical specifications and features of each

S3

Amazon Simple Storage Service (S3) is the most prominent and widely used storage service under AWS. It offers object storage at incredibly high availability levels, with stringent security and backups, and is used for everything from websites, backups, and archives to big data implementations.

Unlike EBS, which resembles a traditional file system with directories and files, S3 is an object file system that is flat in nature and stores files within a bucket. Rather than filenames that are organized in layers of directories, all objects are on the same level and use an alpha-numeric key value for an object name, which can be up to 1,024 bytes long. When you create a bucket, you will give it a name that is between 3 and 63 characters in length and must be globally unique within AWS. Each bucket can only exist within a single AWS region, but data can be replicated between multiple regions for improved speed and lower latency for access. By having each bucket only in a single region, regulatory compliance is easier to maintain based on the location of the region, allowing you to also keep your data in specific regions.

As each piece of data is its own object, each can have its own independent configurations, including tier of storage, security settings, backup configurations, etc. This allows S3 to meet any needs of a company for their object storage and maintain any level of granularity necessary.

 EXAM TIP   Remember that bucket names must be globally unique within AWS, and each bucket can only exist within one region.

S3 Storage Classes   S3 offers four storage classes for users to pick from, depending on their particular needs. Storage classes are set at the object level, and a bucket for a user may contain objects using any of the storage classes concurrently. Figure 4-8 shows each type of S3 storage class and their key specifications.

- **S3 Standard**   Used for commonly accessed data and is optimized for high-throughput and low-latency service. Used widely for cloud applications, websites, content distribution, and data analytics. Encryption is supported for data both at rest and in transit and is resilient to the loss of an entire Availability Zone.

- **S3 Intelligent-Tiering**   Best used for data where usage patterns are unknown or may change over time. This class works by spanning objects across two tiers: one that is optimized for frequent access and the other for lesser access. For a small monitoring fee, AWS will automatically move an object between the two tiers based on access. If an object is not accessed for 30 days, it is automatically moved to the lower-cost tier. Once it is accessed, it is moved back and the clock starts anew. Use of this tier allows users to save money without having to manually monitor and update classes.

- **S3 Standard-Infrequent Access**   Ideally used where access will be infrequent for an object, but when access is requested, a quick response is necessary. This is often used for backups and disaster recovery files that are not accessed with any regularity, but when needed there is an immediacy requirement.

Performance across the S3 Storage Classes

	S3 Standard	S3 Intelligent-Tiering*	S3 Standard-IA	S3 One Zone-IA†	S3 Glacier	S3 Glacier Deep Archive
Designed for durability	99.999999999% (11 9's)	99.999999999% (11 9's)	99.999999999% (11 9's)	99.999999999% (11 9's)	99.999999999% (11 9's)	99.999999999% (11 9's)
Designed for availability	99.99%	99.9%	99.9%	99.5%	99.99%	99.99%
Availability SLA	99.9%	99%	99%	99%	99.9%	99.9%
Availability Zones	≥3	≥3	≥3	1	≥3	≥3
Minimum capacity charge per object	N/A	N/A	128KB	128KB	40KB	40KB
Minimum storage duration charge	N/A	30 days	30 days	30 days	90 days	180 days
Retrieval fee	N/A	N/A	per GB retrieved	per GB retrieved	per GB retrieved	per GB retrieved
First byte latency	milliseconds	milliseconds	milliseconds	milliseconds	select minutes or hours	select hours
Storage type	Object	Object	Object	Object	Object	Object
Lifecycle transitions	Yes	Yes	Yes	Yes	Yes	Yes

Figure 4-8   The S3 storage classes and their key technical specifications and features

- **S3 One Zone-Infrequent Access**   Ideal for data that is infrequently used, requires quick access when it is accessed, but does not require the robust fault tolerance and replication of other S3 classes. Rather than being spread across the typical three Availability Zones, objects under this storage class are housed on a single Availability Zone. This realizes costs savings for users, as it is cheaper than other S3 storage classes that span multiple Availability Zones.

S3 Permissions   AWS S3 offers three different layers of permissions and security controls on S3 objects: bucket, user, and object access control lists.

With bucket policies, security policies are applied at the level of the bucket. These policies can apply to all objects within the bucket or just some objects. For example, for a private bucket that you desire to only allow internal access to objects, a bucket-level policy can be applied that automatically protects every object within it. However, if you have a mix of objects in your bucket, you may have some that are protected to specific users for access, while others, such as those used for public web pages, are open and available to the entire Internet. As the policies are applied to objects, the ability to read, write, and delete objects can all be controlled separately.

Policies can also be applied at the user level. For the accounts you created through the IAM process, you can grant control to those accounts to your S3 objects without the use of a bucket policy. This can be particularly useful where you have users designated to manage objects that may span across multiple buckets and will negate the need to set up bucket policies on each as they are created.

ACLs are legacy methods for controlling access to S3 objects and have mostly been superseded by bucket and user policies. However, they are still available for use, but have distinct limitations as compared to the features available with bucket and user policies and are not recommended to be used for any new setups.

S3 Encryption   When you upload any objects to S3, the data within the object is static and written to storage within the AWS infrastructure. If you upload an object that contains personal or sensitive data, that will now reside in AWS and be accessible based upon the policies and security controls that you have applied to it. While the bucket and user policies you have in place will be applied to those objects, it is possible to upload data that should be protected and somehow slips through your policies for various reasons.

To add another layer of security, especially for those objects that contain sensitive data and are instead to be used for archiving and backups, encryption can also be applied to the data object before it is stored in S3. As this encryption pertains to stored objects, it would be classified as encryption at rest and it can be implemented at either the server side or client side.

With server-side encryption, S3 will automatically encrypt data objects that you upload before they are stored and will decrypt them when accessed and pass the data back to you. While this is the easiest encryption method to implement with S3, it may not meet your specific needs, as AWS will have access to your data. Since AWS is handling the encryption and decryption, they are also managing the encryption keys and have access to them. This will definitely give a high degree of protection for your data, but depending upon your specific needs, regulatory requirements, or company policies, this may not be a desirable approach for you to use. Typically with server-side encryption AWS will generate the keys to use, but there is also the option for AWS to use a key that you provide. AWS will then use your key to perform encryption, but the user retains ownership over their keys.

With client-side encryption, the data object is encrypted before it is uploaded into S3 and then decrypted after the data is returned back from AWS. With this implementation, AWS does not manage the keys and does not have any access to the encrypted data within the object. The user is responsible for managing the encryption process and their own encryption keys. It is very important for the user to not lose their encryption keys or they will be unable to access their data, but it will provide the most security to the user and assurances that only they can read their data.

S3 Versioning   By default, when you update an object in S3, it overwrites and replaces what you previously had uploaded. In many cases this is fine, but it puts the responsibility on the user to ensure they have a backup copy of the object or to otherwise preserve the previous copy. Without doing so, once they have uploaded a new copy, whatever existed before is gone.

A way to mitigate this problem, and to alleviate the need to actively preserve the data yourself, you can enable versioning on an S3 bucket. Versioning can only be enabled at the bucket level and applies to all objects within the bucket. Once you have it enabled, when you upload a new copy of an object, S3 will preserve the previous copy. The same happens when you delete an object. It is marked as deleted but is actually still available, though not through the usual means to access the object.

One thing to note, with versioning enabled, you will incur additional costs as each new version is maintained and adds to your overall storage footprint. You can manually delete version archives of an object or use automated methods to do so. Once you have enabled versioning, there is no default limitation to the number of versions that are retained. If you have some objects that are updated regularly, the number of copies and costs can quickly increase.

S3 Object Life Cycle To help manage versioning in AWS S3, the service provides automation tools, called actions, to handle how versions are stored and when they are removed from the system. This will be particularly useful as the number of objects you have increases or with objects that are regularly updated and will begin to accrue a large number of versions.

The first type of action is a transition action. A transition action will move S3 objects to a different storage class after it reaches a certain age. This will allow you to move objects to cheaper storage after they have been stored for a time frame that you specify and allow you to save costs by using cheaper storage. For example, if you are uploading archives of data, you can allow them to stay in Standard storage for 30 days and then automatically move to Standard-IA at that point. However, make sure you properly provision and use buckets based on the type of usage of the objects. If you have objects such as web content that is stored in S3, you will not likely want them to transition to slower and cheaper storage. If you are using objects for archives, then using a transition would make perfect sense. A strategy to manage this would be through the use of different buckets, as transition actions are done at the bucket level.

The second type of action is an expiration action. This action will automatically expire and remove objects once they reach a certain date. While you may not want to apply this to typical data objects, it is very useful to use with versioning enabled. You can configure the action to automatically remove versions after they reach a certain age, such as 90 days. This would allow you to keep versioning in place to prevent the accidental overwriting and loss of data from previous copies but prevent the continual accrual of previous copies of data objects and the associated increased costs that go with them.

With either transition or expiration actions, they are configured and applied at the bucket level, not the individual object.

S3 Glacier and S3 Glacier Deep

S3 Glacier is a special type of S3 storage that is intended to be a secure solution for long-term data archiving and backups. As compared to regular S3 storage options, Glacier is offered at significant cost savings. These savings are much greater when compared to the costs of on-premises storage solutions for long-term archiving. Depending on retrieval needs, S3 Glacier Deep is a subset of Glacier that is intended for the longest-term storage with the least likely needs for retrieval.

S3 Glacier has three different service offerings to meet varying requirements from users, along with two options for S3 Glacier Deep. Which option is chosen will dictate the costs associated with the service.

The three retrieval options for S3 Glacier are

- **Expedited**   Offers retrieval options that will typically return within one to five minutes. This is the appropriate choice for archived data that may need to be accessed frequently or with data that will have business requirements for very quick retrieval when requested.
- **Standard**   Offers retrieval options that will typically return in three to five hours. This is an appropriate choice for typical archives and backups that do not have a need for immediacy in retrieval.
- **Bulk**   Offers retrieval times of 5 to 12 hours and is the best option for very large retrievals.

With S3 Glacier Deep, there are two options for retrieval times that range between 12 and 48 hours for data access.

One of the key features of S3 Glacier has to do with security and regulatory compliance of archives. S3 Glacier uses powerful encryption that is standard across AWS and integrates with CloudTrail to provide full logging and auditing of all actions taken against archived volumes. The systems in place with the S3 Glacier service meet or exceed regulatory requirements from most major global organizations, including PCI-DSS, HIPAA, FedRAMP, GDPR, and FISMA.

AWS Storage Gateway

The AWS Storage Gateway provides storage for hybrid cloud services that gives access to your on-premises resources to the full array of storage services in AWS. This enables a customer to extend their storage capabilities into AWS seamlessly and with very low latency. A common usage of Storage Gateway is for customers to use AWS to store backups of images from their on-premises environment, or to use the AWS Cloud storage to back their file shares. Many customers also utilize Storage Gateway as a key component to their disaster recovery strategy and planning.

The Storage Gateway is designed to interact with the most commonly used storage protocols, such as iSCSI, NFS, and SMB, to simplify integration with existing systems and processes. The Storage Gateway offers three types of gateways that each serve different purposes: file, tape, and volume.

File gateway is used either for backups or storing of actual application data files to AWS. It works by providing a local cache of storage that is then synced to AWS S3 storage via SMB or NFS file stores. It can be used for storage of files for on-premises systems and works much the same way as OneDrive or iCloud, where local files are synchronized to the cloud for backup purposes. It can also be used in hybrid cloud implementations where both on-premises and EC2 systems in AWS both need access to the same files.

Tape gateway provides a method for customers to utilize AWS storage systems in lieu of tape-based systems for backups. It can integrate with already used systems that customers already have and allow the uploading of tape images to AWS for storing instead of maintaining legacy tape systems in data centers, along with the hardware and facilities costs associated with them.

Volume gateway facilitates the usage of AWS-based iSCSI block storage volumes for on-premises applications. It allows for the storing of files in AWS with a local cache. Customers can also utilize snapshots for backup or disaster recovery purposes.

AWS Backup

AWS Backup provides backup services for all AWS services. It provides a single resource to configure backup policies and monitor their usage and success across any services that you have allocated. This allows administrators to access a single location for all backup services without having to separately configure and monitor on a per-service basis across AWS. From the AWS Backup console, users can fully automate backups and perform operations such as encryption and auditing. AWS Backup has been certified as compliant with many regulatory requirements such as HIPAA, PCI, and ISO, making compliance and the generation of reports trivial.

AWS Backup can also be leveraged in conjunction with the AWS Storage Gateway to provide backups in hybrid cloud implementations for on-premises resources. This functionality can be used as part of a disaster recovery plan, as backup images can easily be restored to on-premises systems or in the AWS Cloud. The same backup policies and automations that are available with AWS services are also available through the Storage Gateway and in hybrid implementations, along with the same benefits of compliance with regulatory requirements.

AWS Snow

AWS Snow is designed for offering compute and storage capabilities to those organizations or places that are outside the areas where AWS regions and resources operate. Snow is based on hardware devices that contain substantial compute and storage resources that can be used both as devices for data processing away from the cloud and as a means to get data into and out of AWS. This is particularly useful in situations where high-speed or reliable networking is not possible.

AWS Snow comes in three different tiers: AWS Snowcone, AWS Snowball, and AWS Snowmobile. All three tiers use 256-bit encryption.

AWS Snowcone is a small hardware device that is easily portable, weighing about 4.5 pounds and measuring 9 inches long, 6 inches wide, and 3 inches tall. It includes 8TB of useable storage and contains 2 vCPUs of compute power, along with 4GB of memory. It has two 1/10 Gbit network interfaces, as well as Wi-Fi capabilities, and can operate on battery power.

AWS Snowball is a larger device that comes in two flavors, one focused on storage and one focused on compute. As opposed to the smaller Snowcone device, the Snowball device weighs 49.7 pounds and measures 28.3 inches long, 10.6 inches wide, and 15.5 inches tall. The model focused on storage has 80TB of useable storage, 40vCPUs, and 80GB of memory. The model focused on compute has 42TB of usable storage, 42vCPUs, and 208GB of memory. Both models feature two 10-Gbit network interfaces, a 25 Gbit interface, and a 100 Gbit interface, but unlike the Snowcone device, they do not have Wi-Fi support.

Lastly is the Snowmobile service, which is used exclusively for the transfer of very large data sets between AWS and outside storage, typically an external data center. The Snowmobile is a 45-foot ruggedized shipping container that is outfitted with 100 petabytes of storage capacity. It is driven to the site of the customer and connected for data transfer. It is then transported to an AWS data center, connected to the network, and data is transferred into the Amazon S3 service. The container is secured during transport through multiple physical and logical means, including encryption, environmental protection, and a security team escort.

Compute Services

With any system or application, you need an underlying compute infrastructure to actually run your code, content, or services. AWS offers the ability through EC2 to run full virtual instances that you maintain control over and can customize as much as you like, as well as managed environments that allow you to just upload your content or code and be quickly running, without having to worry about the underlying environment.

EC2

Amazon Elastic Compute Cloud (EC2) is the main offering for virtual servers in the cloud. It allows users to create and deploy compute instances that they will retain full control over and offers a variety of configuration options for resources.

Amazon Machine Images   Amazon Machine Images (AMIs) are the basis of virtual compute instances in AWS. An image is basically a data object that is a bootable virtual machine and can be deployed throughout the AWS infrastructure. AMIs can be either those offered by AWS through their Quick Start options, those offered by vendors through the AWS Marketplace, or those created by users for their own specific needs.

The AWS Quick Start offers virtual machines from many popular vendor flavors. There are over three dozen in the Quick Start menu and include Microsoft Windows, Red Hat Enterprise Linux (RHEL), Ubuntu Linux, or AWS's own version of Linux called AWS Linux. Each of these offerings has multiple versions available. When you look through the Quick Start options, you will notice that many are available as part of the Free Tier offerings that we are using with our test accounts. These will all be clearly labeled as "Free tier eligible," as shown in Figure 4-9.

Many of the Linux offerings will be free to use. However, offerings such as Microsoft Windows and RHEL will incur licensing charges that will be applied once an instance is launched. The menu offers different versions of images that are also optimized for specific uses, such as those built specifically for containers or for hosting Microsoft SQL Server. For each image presented, you will notice that some are listed specifically for offering SSD storage or different OS release levels or versions.

Apart from the images offered under the Quick Start menu, the AWS Marketplace offers images from many vendors for their specific products. For example, you will find images from companies such as SAP that will offer fully configured images for their software platforms that are ready to deploy. When you select an image from the Marketplace, you may have the option of a trial period to see if it will work for your needs before you incur costs from the vendor. Pricing for images from the Marketplace will be divided into two costs. The first cost will be the charge from the vendor for the use of the image itself, specifically licensing costs. The second cost will be the EC2 costs of hosting the image and the resources it requires from the AWS services perspective. The two combined will

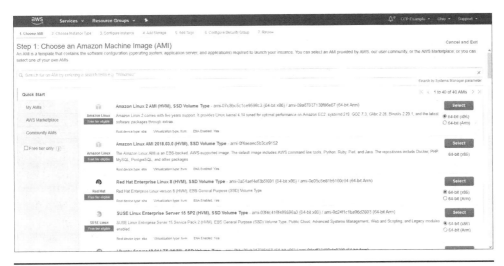

Figure 4-9 The Quick Start menu showing the types of images available. Notice the "Free tier eligible" flags

be the actual cost of using the image. Within the Marketplace you will also find an enormous number of community images that are offered by others who have built and configured them. Some of these are from actual companies or development groups, but others may be offered by the individuals that created them. Take special care with the use of community images and the responsibilities you will be taking on using and supporting them going forward if they are not maintained actively or if the creator takes no responsibility for their use.

EXAM TIP Remember that costs for Marketplace applications will be presented as two costs. The licensing costs from the vendor for use of the image, as well as the EC2 costs for hosting it and the compute/storage resources it will consume.

Lastly, you have the ability to create your own images for use in AWS. This is done by taking a snapshot of the EBS storage volume you have created and configured, which will then be available to you to create new instances from. This is particularly useful when you want to use a base image and then install and configure your own software on top of it. Once you have the image where you need it to be, you can take a snapshot and then reuse as needed, without having to apply any software installations or configurations on each new instance. By creating your own instance, you will be taking the responsibility for patching and managing security issues for it going forward.

EC2 Instance Types   EC2 instance types are where the underlying hardware resources are married with the type of image you are using. The instance type will dictate the type of CPU used, how many virtual CPUs (vCPUs) it has, how much memory, the type of storage used, network bandwidth, and the underlying EBS bandwidth.

Purpose	Instance Types
General Purpose	A1, T3, T3a, T2, M6g, M5, M5a, M5n, M4
Compute Optimized	C6g, C5, C5a, C5n, C4
Memory Optimized	R6g, R5, R5a, R5n, R4, X1e, X1, High Memory, z1d
Accelerated Computing	P3, P2, Inf1, G4, G3, F1
Storage Optimized	I3, I3en, D2, H1

Table 4-2 The Instance Types and Their Purposes

Instance types are categorized by their intended purpose, and then several instance types are offered with base configuration and specifications within it, as shown in Table 4-2.

You can find all of the instance types and tables of all configuration offerings at https://aws.amazon.com/ec2/instance-types/. This will break down each instance type, information about the specific types of processors it uses, network information, storage information, and any other specifics related to it. For example, Figure 4-10 shows the "A1" instance type from the "General Purpose" category and its technical specifications.

A1	T3	T3a	T2	M6g	M5	M5a	M5n	M4

Amazon EC2 A1 instances deliver significant cost savings and are ideally suited for scale-out and Arm-based workloads that are supported by the extensive Arm ecosystem. A1 instances are the first EC2 instances powered by AWS Graviton Processors that feature 64-bit Arm Neoverse cores and custom silicon designed by AWS.

Features:

- Custom built AWS Graviton Processor with 64-bit Arm Neoverse cores
- Support for Enhanced Networking with Up to 10 Gbps of Network bandwidth
- EBS-optimized by default
- Powered by the AWS Nitro System, a combination of dedicated hardware and lightweight hypervisor

Instance	vCPU	Mem (GiB)	Storage	Network Performance (Gbps)
a1.medium	1	2	EBS-Only	Up to 10
a1.large	2	4	EBS-Only	Up to 10
a1.xlarge	4	8	EBS-Only	Up to 10
a1.2xlarge	8	16	EBS-Only	Up to 10
a1.4xlarge	16	32	EBS-Only	Up to 10
a1.metal	16*	32	EBS-Only	Up to 10

Figure 4-10 The "A1" instance type and its technical specifications from the "General Purpose" category

EXAM TIP It is not necessary to memorize all of the instance types and which purposes they associate with. However, make sure you know the five main categories/purposes of instance types.

Lightsail

Lightsail is the quickest way to get into AWS for new users. It offers blueprints that will configure fully ready systems and application stacks for you to immediately begin using and deploying your code or data into. Lightsail is fully managed by AWS and is designed to be a one-click deployment model to get you up and running quickly at a low cost.

Since Lightsail is fully managed and configured by AWS, it does not come with the same range offerings and images as EC2 does but will still cover the needs of many customers. If you start using Lightsail and later want to convert to the more powerful and customizable EC2 service, you can convert your Lightsail instances into EC2.

Many of the most popular operating systems, applications, or stacks are available with Lightsail, as shown in Figure 4-11.

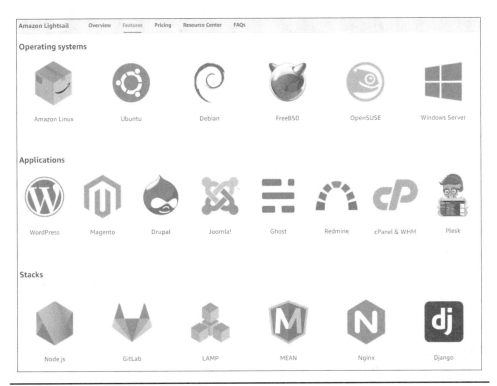

Figure 4-11 The operating systems, applications, and stacks available within the Lightsail service

Elastic Beanstalk

Elastic Beanstalk is designed to be even easier and quicker to get your applications up and running in than Lightsail is. With Elastic Beanstalk, you choose the application platform that your code is written in, such as Java, Node.js, PHP, or .NET. Once you provision the instance you can deploy your code into it and begin running. You only select the platform that you need—you do not select specific hardware or compute resources. AWS will automatically size your instance based on the traffic and compute needs and will upsize and downsize as load changes. Since you are not provisioning specific resources, you are billed for what you consume. This is particularly useful if you are using a web application that experiences a sudden spike in traffic—the AWS service will automatically meet your needs and size accordingly.

Lambda

AWS Lambda is a service for running code for virtually any application or back-end service. All you need to do is upload your code, and there are no systems or resources to manage. The code can be called by services or applications, and you will only incur costs based on the processing time and the number of times your code is called, as well as the memory that you allocate. You will always have the level of resources you need available to run your code without having to provision or monitor anything.

Containers

With typical server models, there is an enormous duplication of resources when replicas of systems are created. When you launch several instances of EC2, each one has its own operating system and underlying functions and services that are needed to run. Before your application code is even used, each instance is consuming a certain amount of compute resources just to exist. A modern approach to this problem has been through the use of containers, such as Docker. This allows a single system instance to host multiple virtual environments within it while leveraging the underlying infrastructure.

In AWS various AMIs are available from the Quick Start that are optimized for the use of container hosting. This allows for a user to pay for a single instance of EC2 but have multiple environments within it and sharing its compute resources. However, if you do not want to have to run EC2 instances, AWS offers two container solutions where you can deploy Docker containers but leverage a managed underlying infrastructure. The two AWS services that facilitate container hosting are the Amazon Elastic Container Service (ECS) and the Amazon Elastic Kubernetes Service (EKS). Both services will allow for the hosting of containers, the only difference being that EKS is the AWS-specific implementation of the popular open-source Kubernetes system.

Databases

As many modern applications are heavily dependent on databases, AWS has several database service offerings that will fit any type of use needed, ranging from relational databases to data warehousing. AWS provides robust tools for migrating databases from legacy and on-premises systems into AWS, as well as transitioning between different database services.

Database Models

Databases follow two general models. They can be either relational or nonrelational. Which one you use is entirely dependent on the needs of your application and the type of data it is accessing and dependent on.

Relational databases are often referred to as structured data. A relational database utilizes a primary key to track a unique record, but then can have many data elements associated with it. For example, with a company, a primary key may be a personnel number, with then many attached elements such as name, address, date of birth, phone number, etc. The concept of it being structured data is based on how each element must be predefined before it is populated, both with a name for the field and also what type of data it will contain. For example, a field for such a personnel number would be defined as a numeric field, and any attempt to put different data types into it would result in errors. This structure makes it possible to run very complex and layered queries against the database to return results to applications. You can run queries against any of the fields to obtain results; you are not restricted to queries just against the primary key. Within AWS, the Amazon Relational Database Service (RDS) is the primary relational database service.

Nonrelational databases are referred to as unstructured data. While their tables also utilize a primary key, the data paired with that primary key is not restricted to the type of data. This allows applications to store a variety of data within their tables. However, it also restricts queries against these tables to the primary key value, as the paired data could be in different formats and structures and would not be efficient or stable to query from applications generally. Having queries restricted to the primary key also makes these databases extremely fast to query as compared to relational databases. For applications that must handle massive amounts of data and need the fastest possible results, especially where only limited optimized queries are required, nonrelational databases are optimal. Within AWS, the DynamoDB service is the primary example of a nonrelational database and the massive throughput it is capable of.

 EXAM TIP Make sure you understand the differences between relational and nonrelational databases and what they are used for, especially the key aspects of how they may be searched.

AWS Database Migration Service

That AWS Database Migration Service (DMS) is a tool for migrating data into AWS databases from existing databases with minimal downtime or other interruptions. The DMS can move data from most of the popular and widely used databases into the various AWS database services while the source system remains fully operational. DMS can do migrations where the source and destination databases are the same, such as moving from Microsoft SQL server from another location into a Microsoft SQL server database in AWS, but it can also perform migrations where they differ, such as moving from a Microsoft SQL server into the various AWS database services. Migrations can also be performed within AWS from source to destination. In either instance, data can be continuously synchronized from the source into AWS, allowing production cutover at whatever time best fits the needs for the system. When DMS is used to migrate data into an AWS database service, DMS is free to use for a period of six months.

More information about DMS, including detailed information on use cases for migration from prominent companies, can be found at https://aws.amazon.com/dms/.

 NOTE The availability of DMS is a great opportunity for any users that have been contemplating changing back-end databases but have been cautious about the level of effort involved in the actual migration of data.

Amazon Relational Database Service

Amazon RDS is an umbrella service that incorporates several different kinds of database systems. Each system is fully managed by AWS and is optimized within the AWS infrastructure for memory, performance, and I/O. All aspects of database management, such as provisioning, configuration, maintenance, performance monitoring, and backups, are handled by AWS, which allows the user to fully focus on their applications and data.

The current offerings from AWS RDS are

- Microsoft SQL Server
- Oracle
- MariaDB
- MySQL
- PostgreSQL
- Amazon Aurora

Aligned with other AWS services, RDS will only incur costs for the resources you are actually using. You can also modify the allocated storage and compute resources provisioned for your RDS instances at any time and without downtime, either through the Management Console or through API calls, allowing for automation. RDS runs within the same global infrastructure as other AWS services, allowing for RDS services to be spread across multiple regions and Availability Zones like EC2, either with a standby instance or through the use of read-only replicas, depending on the requirements of your applications.

RDS runs within VPC, providing all of the security layers from it. It also allows on-premises applications to access RDS instances through your VPC and security group rules over encrypted IPsec channels and inherit all of the security controls within AWS such as encrypted storage.

You can get more detailed information about RDS and some information about actual implementations from some prominent companies at https://aws.amazon.com/rds.

Amazon Aurora Aurora is a subset of Amazon RDS that is compatible with both MySQL and PostgreSQL databases. It combines the features and simplicity of open-source databases with the robust management and security of AWS services. Aurora leverages the AWS infrastructure to offer highly optimized and fast database services, along with the robust security and reliability of AWS.

Aurora is a subset of the Amazon RDS database service. As such, it can fully leverage all of the automation features of RDS, along with the management of resource provisioning, configuration, and backups. It also inherits the fault-tolerance aspects of RDS, as it is distributed across multiple Availability Zones and continually backed up to S3 storage. Aurora can handle databases up to 64TB in size per instance and will only incur costs for those resources actually in use.

With Aurora being completely compatible with both MySQL and PostgreSQL, migration from existing on-premises systems or other virtual systems from both technologies is trivial. Aurora migrations can be fully leveraged through the AWS Database Migration Service.

DynamoDB

DynamoDB is the AWS key-value and document database solution for those applications that do not need a SQL or relational database but do need extremely high performance and scalable access to their data. As with other AWS services, DynamoDB is fully configured, maintained, and secured by AWS, so all the user needs to do is create a table and populate their data.

DynamoDB replicates tables automatically across multiple AWS regions to optimize performance and serve data from the closest location possible to the requests. AWS also offers memory caching through the DynamoDB Accelerator service for those applications that need the fastest possible access to data.

As DynamoDB is fully managed by AWS, there is nothing to configure other than populating your data. As there are no resources to provision, it will automatically scale up and down to meet your needs and adjust for capacity. High availability and fault tolerance are already built into the service, so they do not need to be provisioned or managed by the user, nor do any changes need to be made to application code to leverage either feature.

From a security standpoint, DynamoDB is fully encrypted and allows for granular access controls on tables. It is automatically backed up without any downtime or performance issues for applications and keeps 35 days of recovery points.

You can learn more about DynamoDB, along with case studies from many different market sectors and industries, at https://aws.amazon.com/dynamodb.

Amazon Redshift

Redshift is a cloud-based data warehouse solution offered by AWS. Unlike traditional on-premises data warehouses, Redshift leverages AWS storage to any capacity that is needed by a company, either now or into the future. Organizations only will incur costs for the storage they actually use, as well as the compute power they need to do analysis and retrieve data. Typically, an organization must spend money on having sufficient capacity and continually add both compute and storage infrastructure to support growth and expansion, resulting in expenses for idle systems. Redshift also has the advantage of costs being independent between storage and compute. This will properly fit resources to the needs of an organization that might need massive amounts of storage but uses little computing power to analyze it, along with the opposite—organizations that might not use as much data but continually run reports and queries. As an organization's needs grow in either aspect, Redshift will automatically scale the resources available as needed.

Automation

In AWS, automation is essential to enable systems to be rapidly and correctly deployed and configured.

CloudFormation

CloudFormation implements an automated way to model infrastructure and resources within AWS via either a text file or through the use of programming languages. This allows administrators to build out templates for the provisioning of resources that can then be repeated in a secure and reliable manner. As you build new systems or replicate services, you can be assured that they are being done in a consistent and uniform manner, negating the process of building out from a base image and then having to apply different packages, configurations, or scripts to fully build up systems to a ready state. With the use of file-based templates, CloudFormation allows infrastructure and services to be treated as code. This allows administrators to use version control to track changes to the infrastructure and use build pipelines to deploy the infrastructure changes. CloudFormation not only helps with infrastructure, it can also help build and deploy your applications!

End-User Computing

AWS offers powerful tools to organizations to provide end-user computing such as virtual desktops and access to applications or internally protected websites.

WorkSpaces

Amazon WorkSpaces is a Desktop as a Service (DaaS) implementation that is built, maintained, configured, and secured through AWS as a managed service. WorkSpaces offers both Windows and Linux desktop solutions that can be quickly deployed anywhere throughout the AWS global infrastructure. As many organizations have moved to virtual desktop infrastructure (VDI) solutions, WorkSpaces enables them to offer the same solutions to their users without the need to actually purchase and maintain the hardware required for the VDI infrastructure, as well as the costs of managing and securing it. With the global nature of AWS infrastructure, the virtual desktops for users are available anywhere at any time and from any supported device. From the standpoint of security, WorkSpaces is fully encrypted and operates within your VPC. Users' data is maintained within the WorkSpaces service and is not present on the actual devices used to access it, providing additional security should those devices be lost or compromised.

AppStream

AppStream is a service for providing managed and streaming applications via AWS. By streaming applications, the need to download and install applications is removed, as they will be run through a web browser. This eliminates the need for an organization to distribute software and support the installation and configuration of it to their users. This can be particularly useful for organizations like academic institutions that can offer a suite of software to their students without the need for them to actually obtain and install it, while also making it available to them from any device with network access. Another powerful use of AppStream is for demos and trial software, especially if it is continually updated and patched, as the users will always have the latest version when launching the application. Costs are only incurred when applications are actually accessed, saving organizations from the need to purchase sometimes vast libraries of software that may in some instances only be used sparingly by their users.

WorkLink

WorkLink offers users the ability to access internal applications through the use of mobile devices. Traditionally this access would be controlled and secured through the use of technologies like virtual private networks (VPNs) or through the use of mobile device management (MDM) utilities. Both of these technologies must be already installed and configured on a user's device before they can be used, which can make access difficult for users that may need to use a variety of devices, or even for users that get new devices and will be hampered in terms of productivity until the new device can be configured. Through the use of WorkLink, users will access a web browser that can be used on any mobile device and obtain easy access to their internal systems. For optimal security, the content is first rendered on a browser running within the AWS infrastructure, with the resulting display then sent to the user's devices. This eliminates processing being done on the actual device and removes the potential for local caching or compromise. Since costs are only incurred when WorkLink is actually used, an organization can realize significant savings by no longer needing to operate and support VPN or MDM technologies.

Technology Support

For technical support, AWS users have access to the full range of documentation, the AWS Knowledge Center, whitepapers, and support forums. For users with a Developer, Business, or Enterprise support plan, you also have the ability to submit technical support cases through the AWS Support Center, found at https://console.aws.amazon.com/support.

AWS technical support covers AWS services and their administration, as well as deployment support and troubleshooting operation issues. There is also support for many third-party applications that have agreements with AWS and are officially offered through AWS.

AWS technical support does not cover code development and debugging of code. Technical support will assist with the use of development tools and services, but not with the actual code written by users, nor will they provide assistance with tuning database queries.

AWS also offers Professional Services, which provides a specialized team with deep AWS knowledge and experience to supplement your team and help you realize outcomes and the best approaches to take within AWS. You can find out more about Professional Services at https://aws.amazon.com/professional-services/.

Chapter Review

In this chapter we covered the main AWS services and the key concepts and components of each. While these are not all of the AWS services, they are the main and most popular ones. For each service we covered how AWS can offer improvements in both services and costs as compared to legacy data centers, as well as tools that AWS has implemented to allow for an easy and efficient migration into AWS from other environments, as well as tools that AWS offers for development and even end-user computing. We also covered resources available to users for technical support of AWS services.

Exercise 4-1: Create an S3 Bucket

In this exercise we will create an S3 bucket. There are no costs associated with having an empty bucket.

1. Log in to the Management Console with your root account at https://aws.amazon.com.

2. Select the Services dropdown in the upper-right corner, then select S3 under Storage.

3. Click the Create Bucket button.

    a. Enter a bucket name. Remember, this name must be unique across all of AWS, so pick a name that is unlikely to be used by anyone else, or add a string of numbers to the end of a name to reach a unique value.

    b. Select a region to create your bucket.

    c. Click Next.

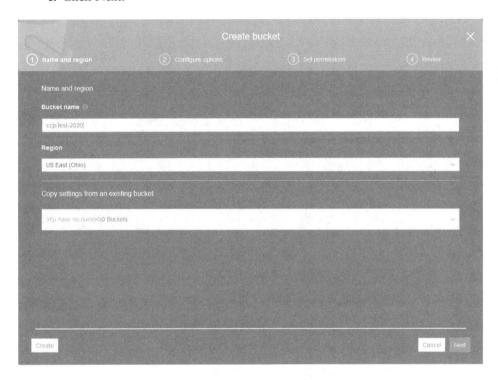

4. On the Configure Options screen you will be presented with many of the options we discussed with S3.

    a. Under Versioning check the box to create versions of objects.

    b. Under Encryption check the box to automatically encrypt objects when they are stored in S3. You will be presented with the choice of using AES-256 or AWS-KMS encryption. Leave the default selected for AES-256.

    c. Click Next.

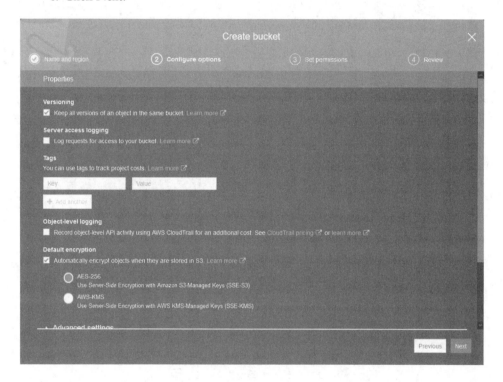

5. On the Set Permissions screen you will be able to configure the default permission on any objects created within your bucket.

    a. By default, the Block *All* Public Access button is selected. Leave it selected for this exercise.

    b. Click Next.

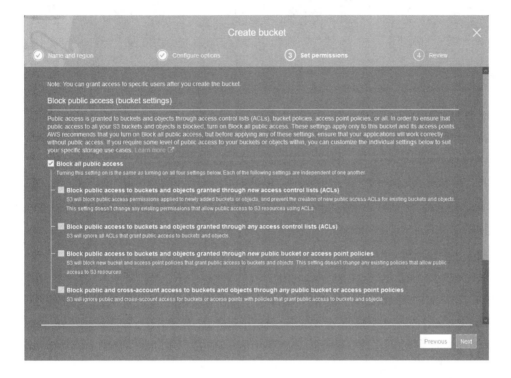

6. You will now be presented with the Review screen that will show all of the options you have selected on the previous wizard panels.

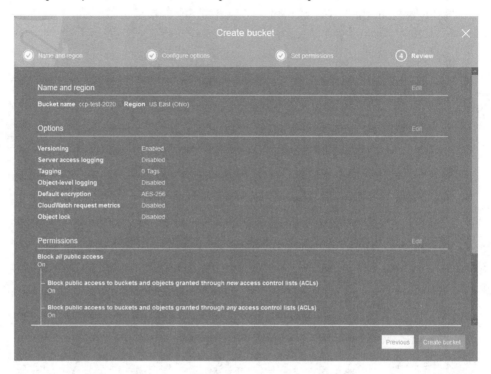

7. Click Create Bucket.

8. You will now see that your bucket has been created successfully.

Exercise 4-2: Use the AWS CLI

For a brief introduction to the AWS CLI, we are going to use it to show the bucket that you just created in the previous exercise.

1. Visit the AWS CLI page to download and install the plug-in appropriate to your platform. This can be found at https://aws.amazon.com/cli. In the upper-right corner are links for each type of supported operating system.

2. Click on the one appropriate to your operating system, allow the file to download, and then run the installer. This will add features to your built-in CLI to work with AWS.

3. Once the installer is complete, open a command line interface window.

4. We first need to configure the CLI to access your instance.

5. On the CLI window, type **aws configure** and press ENTER.

6. You will be prompted for the AWS access key ID for a user within your IAM. You will also need the AWS secret access key for the user.

   a. To get the keys, open the IAM console at https://console.aws.amazon.com/iam/home.

   b. Log in with your root user credentials.

   c. Click on the Users tab on the left column.

   d. Click on the user that you created under IAM previously.

   e. Then click on the Security Credentials tab.

   f. Under Access Keys, click the Create Access Key button.

   g. This will display a window with the access key and secret key. *Do not* close this window until you are done with the AWS configure command on the CLI, as you can only display the secret key once. If you accidently do close it, you can create a new secret key.

7. Copy and paste the AWS access key ID from the Security Credentials window and press ENTER.

8. Click on Show for the security key and copy and paste into the CLI window for the AWS Secret Access Key and press ENTER.

9. You will be prompted for a region. This can always be changed later, so just enter **us-east-2** for these purposes.

10. For the Default Output Format, enter **Text** and press ENTER.

11. AWS CLI is now configured for use with your account.

12. To show the bucket you previously created, enter **aws s3 ls** and press ENTER.

13. You should see an output like this:

    C:\WINDOWS\system32>aws s3 ls
    2020-08-24 00:29:22 ccp-test-2020

This has been just a brief demonstration of what you can do with the AWS CLI. Please look around the documentation and the various things you can do with different services.

Questions

1. Which of the following is not one of the purposes of instance types under EC2?

   A. Compute optimized

   B. Storage optimized

   C. Accelerated computing

   D. Network optimized

2. Which AWS service allows a user to run code in the AWS infrastructure without having to specifically provision resources?

   A. Snow

   B. Redshift

   C. Lambda

   D. AppStream

3. When creating an S3 bucket, how many versions are maintained by default for objects?

   A. None

   B. Unlimited

   C. 1

   D. 64

4. Which AWS database service is the data warehousing service?

   A. Aurora

   B. Redshift

   C. DynamoDB

   D. RDS

5. Which AWS service will inspect web traffic to your applications and apply rules and security controls based on the contents of the traffic?

   A. CloudWatch

   B. Shield

   C. WAF

   D. CloudTrail

6. Which AWS service provides central collection and auditing for event and log data from your AWS services?

   A. CloudTrail

   B. CloudWatch

    C. Lightsail

    D. WorkLink

7. Which AWS service is a Desktop as a Service offering for virtual desktop computing?

    A. Aurora

    B. AppStream

    C. Lambda

    D. WorkSpaces

8. Which AWS service is a developer tool that fully implements the popular Git utility?

    A. CodeBuild

    B. CodeDeploy

    C. CodeCommit

    D. AWS Git

9. If your application is moving to AWS and is currently built on MySQL, which AWS service would you migrate your data into?

    A. Aurora

    B. DynamoDB

    C. RedShift

    D. Lambda

10. Where would you find AMIs provided by vendors for use within AWS?

    A. myAMIs menu under EC2

    B. AWS Marketplace

    C. AWS AMI Artifact Repository (A3R)

    D. AWS Digital Library (ADL)

Questions and Answers

1. Which of the following is not one of the purposes of instance types under EC2?

    A. Compute optimized

    B. Storage optimized

    C. Accelerated computing

    D. Network optimized

    ☑ **D.** The EC2 service does not utilize a network-optimized purpose of instance types. The instance types are general purpose, compute optimized, storage optimized, accelerated computing, and memory optimized.

2. Which AWS service allows a user to run code in the AWS infrastructure without having to specifically provision resources?

    A. Snow

    B. Redshift

    C. Lambda

    D. AppStream

    ☑ **C.** Lambda allows a user to run code in the AWS infrastructure for application calls or back-end services without provisioning specific compute resources. The Lambda service will provision the necessary resources and bill based on the amount of processing done and the number of calls made to code.

3. When creating an S3 bucket, how many versions are maintained by default for objects?

    A. None

    B. Unlimited

    C. 1

    D. 64

    ☑ **A.** When a new bucket is created, versioning is not turned on automatically unless it is chosen as an option during creation.

4. Which AWS database service is the data warehousing service?

    A. Aurora

    B. Redshift

    C. DynamoDB

    D. RDS

    ☑ **B.** Redshift is the AWS data warehousing service that allows for virtually unlimited storage of data and extremely fast queries.

5. Which AWS service will inspect web traffic to your applications and apply rules and security controls based on the contents of the traffic?

    A. CloudWatch

    B. Shield

    C. WAF

    D. CloudTrail

    ☑ **C.** The AWS Web Application Firewall (WAF) will inspect the content of web traffic and apply rules and security controls to it.

6. Which AWS service provides central collection and auditing for event and log data from your AWS services?

   A. CloudTrail

   B. CloudWatch

   C. Lightsail

   D. WorkLink

   ☑ **A.** CloudTrail centralizes the collection of event and security logs into a system that allows auditing and compliance of all user activities within your AWS account.

7. Which AWS service is a Desktop as a Service offering for virtual desktop computing?

   A. Aurora

   B. AppStream

   C. Lambda

   D. WorkSpaces

   ☑ **D.** WorkSpaces offers fully managed and maintained virtual desktops that can be accessed by users from anywhere and provide access into the VPC and applications for your organization.

8. Which AWS service is a developer tool that fully implements the popular Git utility?

   A. CodeBuild

   B. CodeDeploy

   C. CodeCommit

   D. AWS Git

   ☑ **C.** The AWS CodeCommit service is a Git-compliant repository that is fully secured and managed by AWS and capable of scaling to meet any demand.

9. If your application is moving to AWS and is currently built on MySQL, which AWS service would you migrate your data into?

   A. Aurora

   B. DynamoDB

   C. RedShift

   D. Lambda

   ☑ **A.** Aurora is the MySQL and PostgreSQL implementation of Amazon RDS.

10. Where would you find AMIs provided by vendors for use within AWS?

   A. myAMIs menu under EC2

   B. AWS Marketplace

   C. AWS AMI Artifact Repository (A3R)

   D. AWS Digital Library (ADL)

   ☑ **B.** The AWS Marketplace contains AMIs that are official and supported by the vendor. Many offer free trial periods for users before committing to a purchase.

Billing and Pricing

In this chapter, you will learn the following Domain 4 topics:
- Compare and contrast the various pricing models for AWS
- Recognize the various account structures in relation to AWS billing and pricing
- Identify resources available for billing support

AWS offers many different pricing models across all of their services, with the one unifying fact that costs are only incurred for resources that are provisioned, and only while they are being used. With the complexity of services and all the possible cost points, AWS provides management tools to estimate, plan, and track usage of both services and budgets to allow users to stay on top of their costs. This includes both the AWS Free Tier and paid services.

AWS Free Tier

AWS offers a generous array of services for free under the AWS Free Tier. This allows AWS users to either use a low level of services for free or to try out services before deciding whether or not to actually purchase them.

Categories of Free Offerings

Offerings under the Free Tier fall into one of three categories: always free, 12 months free, or trials. Some services may have offerings in all three types of categories, and it will depend on your needs and goals for using a service as to which is the best option for you.

Services offered under the Free Tier are always changing and can be found at https://aws.amazon.com/free.

Always Free

Services offered in the "always free" category are available to all AWS users and do not carry an expiration date. Depending on the service, the portion that is free can be a static amount, such as storage, or it can be for the amount of usage per month, such as compute services under Lambda.

Here are some examples of the most popular services offered under the "always free" category, as also shown in Figure 5-1.

- **DynamoDB**   Provides 25GB of storage. This also comes with enough read/write capacity allocated to handle up to 200 million requests per month.
- **Lambda**   Up to 1,000,000 free requests per month, including up to 3.2 million seconds of compute time per month.
- **CloudWatch**   Ten custom metrics and ten alarms, as well as 1,000,000 API requests, 5GB of log ingestion, and 5GB of log storage. This also includes three dashboards and up to 50 metrics for each one per month.
- **Glacier**   Up to 10GB of Amazon Glacier retrievals per month for standard retrievals using the Glacier API.
- **Storage Gateway**   First 100GB of usage.
- **Server Migration Service**   Migration of an unlimited number of servers into AWS from on-premises or Microsoft Azure.

Figure 5-1   The top options for the "always free" category of the AWS Free Tier

12 Months Free

Services offered in the "12 months free" category are available free for the first 12 months after account creation. In many instances, they are full AWS services, but offered with certain limitations, such as the amount of storage, number of transactions, or amount of compute time. If you exceed the free portion of these services during those 12 months, you will be billed for the amount in excess.

Here are some examples of the most popular services offered under the "12 months free" category, as shown in Figure 5-2:

- **EC2**   Provides 750 hours per month of compute power. The 750 hours applies to Linux, RHEL, or SLES t2.micro or t3.micro instances or Windows t2.micro or t3.micro. These offerings are dependent on which region is being used.

- **S3**   Provides 5GB of standard storage, including up to 20,000 GET requests and 2,000 PUT requests.

- **RDS**   Provides 750 hours per month of db.t2.micro database usage. This also includes up to 20GB of SSD database storage and 20GB of storage for database backups and snapshots.

- **API Gateway**   One million API calls received per month.

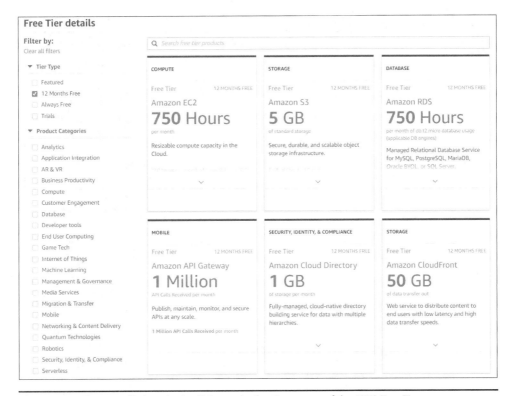

Figure 5-2   The top offerings in the "12 months free" category of the AWS Free Tier

- **CloudFront** Provides 50GB of data transfer out, allowing for up to 2,000,000 HTTP or HTTPS requests.
- **Cloud Directory** Provides 1GB of storage per month, allowing for 10,000 API calls per month.

Trials

Services offered under the "trials" category of the Free Tier at AWS services are available for free for a short period of time after activation. This enables users to test and develop on services to see if they will meet their needs. Once the trial period has elapsed, if you continue to use the services, you will incur charges for them.

Here are some examples of the most popular services offered under the "trials" category, as shown in Figure 5-3:

- **Lightsail** Provides 750 hours for a one-month free trial. This allows a free month trial of what would normally cost $3.50 USD for the Linux/Unix Lightsail platform or the $8 USD Microsoft Windows Lightsail platform.
- **GuardDuty** Thirty days free trial of the Amazon GuardDuty service for intelligent threat detection and monitoring of accounts and workloads.

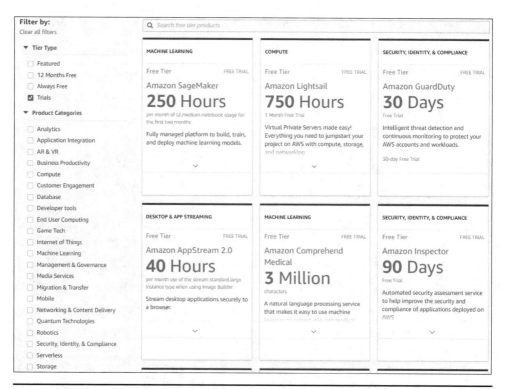

Figure 5-3 The top offerings in the "trial" category of the AWS Free Tier

- **AppStream 2.0** Allows for 40 hours use of the stream.standard.large instance type.
- **Inspector** Ninety-day trial for the security assessment service, covering 90 days or 250 assessments, whichever occurs first.

Use of Services Beyond the Free Tier

Whether you use always-free services, 12-month-free services, or trials, if you exceed the limitations of what is offered free by AWS, you will incur charges for whatever you use beyond that. Left unchecked, it is easy to forget about services that you left running and end up incurring billed services, even potentially very large bills.

You can always find all the information about your services and billing from the AWS Billing Console, found at https://console.aws.amazon.com/billing. The Billing Console main dashboard is shown in Figure 5-4.

AWS will automatically send you e-mail alerts when you are nearing the limits of the Free Tier or when you have exceeded the limits. Unfortunately, the alert e-mails are not customizable, nor do they offer granularity; they are either on or off. If you wish to disable them, you can do so from the Preferences under the Billing Dashboard in the AWS Management Console. By clicking on the Billing Preferences link on the left margin menu, you can either disable the reports completely or set an alternative e-mail address to receive them, as shown in Figure 5-5.

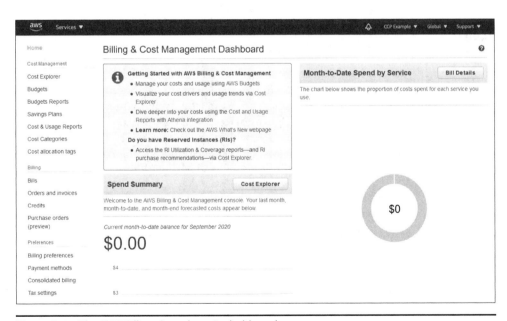

Figure 5-4   The AWS Billing Console main dashboard

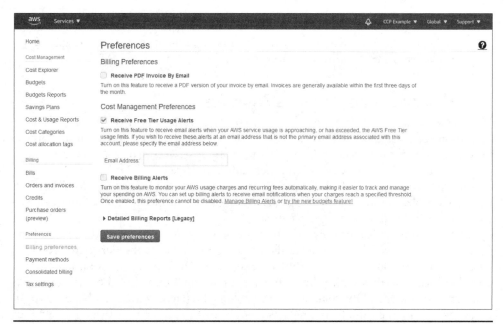

Figure 5-5 The Billing Preferences menu

AWS Service Pricing

Throughout all of the AWS services, a pricing model is based upon paying for usage as you go. When you provision and use services, you will incur costs, but only for the services you are using and while you are using them. There are no minimum purchases or long-term contracts for services, so you can start and stop using them at any time.

With the diversity of AWS services, each service has its own pricing model that is distinct from other services. Even those services within the same category, such as compute, can have very different billing models based on how the service operates. Each service has a different focus for how resources are provisioned, and even within the service, based on the level and type of options you select, pricing can widely vary.

The main consolidated source of pricing for AWS services can be found at https://aws.amazon.com/pricing. This page will provide links to all of the various AWS services and their pricing pages, as shown in Figure 5-6.

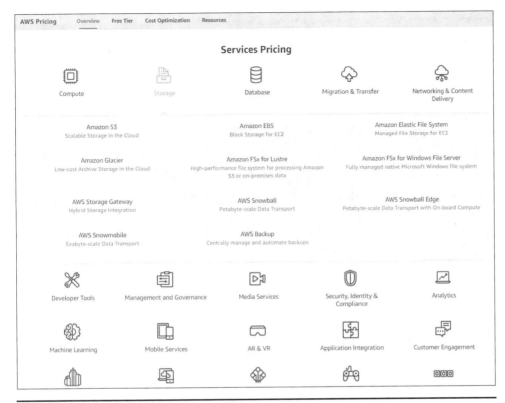

Figure 5-6 The main AWS Pricing page with the Storage category expanded

Following through to the S3 page, you will find the full list of pricing options and options available for S3 storage. To directly go to any pricing page, all services follow the same URL pattern. S3, for example, can be found at https://aws.amazon.com/s3/pricing/. For any service, simply adding "/pricing" to the URL will land you on the pricing page, or you can click on the Pricing option across the top menu bar, as shown in Figure 5-7.

You will also notice on the S3 pricing page an option to select which region you will be provisioning storage in. AWS services can vary slightly in their pricing based on the region selected. The variances tend to be small between regions, but it is always best to check when considering regions—especially as you consume more resources, the variances can start to add up!

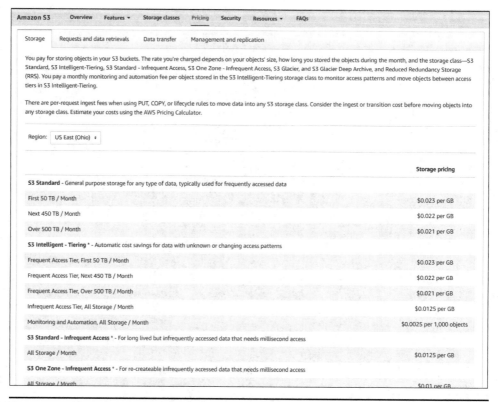

Figure 5-7 The "pricing" table for the Amazon S3 service

You also likely noticed that for S3, there are different tabs for Storage, Requests and Data Retrieval, Data Transfer, and Management and Replication. Since everything with AWS is billed on exactly what services you need, each aspect of pricing is separately itemized. This does add complexity to understanding the overall costs of your services, but it also allows you to fully understand what you are paying for and make informed decisions on what exactly you need and what fits within your budget.

On the bottom of each pricing page, there will be a section for the AWS Free Tier that will explain what is available for that particular service under the Free Tier offerings.

NOTE As with anything in cloud and AWS services, change is always constant. Check the pricing pages regularly, as the pricing models will often change over time and will affect your overall budget. AWS services also offer discounts the more resources you consume. What you pay for a small level of storage or services per unit will decrease as you use more.

AWS Pricing Calculator

The AWS Pricing Calculator services as your one-stop shop for generating estimates for all AWS services. It can be used for a single estimate for one service or can be used to add an entire menu of services to generate a consolidated estimate. This is particularly useful where you can account for all services that an application will need within AWS and be provided with a total cost of ownership (TCO).

A great feature of the Pricing Calculator is that it shows you all the work that goes into arriving at your estimate. By showing all calculations, you can be assured that the estimate is correct, as you can validate it yourself if you like. It also allows you to see the exact cost of each component of pricing. For example, Figure 5-8 shows calculations for an S3 estimate using the following criteria:

- US East (Ohio) region
- S3 Standard storage: 1TB/month
- 200 PUT, COPY, POST, and LIST requests for S3 standard
- 10,000 GET, SELECT, and all other requests for S3 standard

The Pricing Calculator will prompt the user to select a region for those services where region is applicable to pricing. This will allow a correct estimate that takes into account the pricing variations by region and will also ensure that the service the user is looking to provision is available in that region.

For some complex services, with EC2 being a prime example, the calculator will allow for a quick estimate or an advanced estimate, as shown in Figure 5-9. A quick estimate is useful if you have a fairly steady level of resource consumption and want a ballpark estimate based on minimum requirements for an instance. If you have a more complex configuration or known surges in resource utilization, an advanced estimate will give you a much clearer sense of likely charges.

▼ **Show calculations**

Unit conversions
S3 Standard storage: 1 TB per month x 1024 GB in a TB = 1024 GB per month

Pricing calculations
Tiered price for: 1024 GB
1024 GB x 0.0230000000 USD = 23.55 USD
Total tier cost = 23.55 USD (S3 Standard storage cost)
200 PUT requests for S3 Storage x 0.000005 USD per request = 0.001 USD (S3 Standard PUT requests cost)
10,000 GET requests in a month x 0.0000004 USD per request = 0.004 USD (S3 Standard GET requests cost)
23.552 USD + 0.004 USD + 0.001 USD = 23.56 USD (Total S3 Standard Storage, data requests, S3 select cost)
S3 Standard cost (monthly): 23.56 USD

Figure 5-8   Example calculations for a simple S3 estimate

Configure Amazon EC2 Info
Region
US East (Ohio)
Quick estimate
Advanced estimate
EC2 instance specifications Info
Operating system
Linux
Instance type
Enter minimum requirements for each instance:
Search instances by name:
vCPUs
4
Remove
Memory (GiB)
16
Remove
Add requirement
Based on your inputs, this is the lowest-cost EC2 instance:

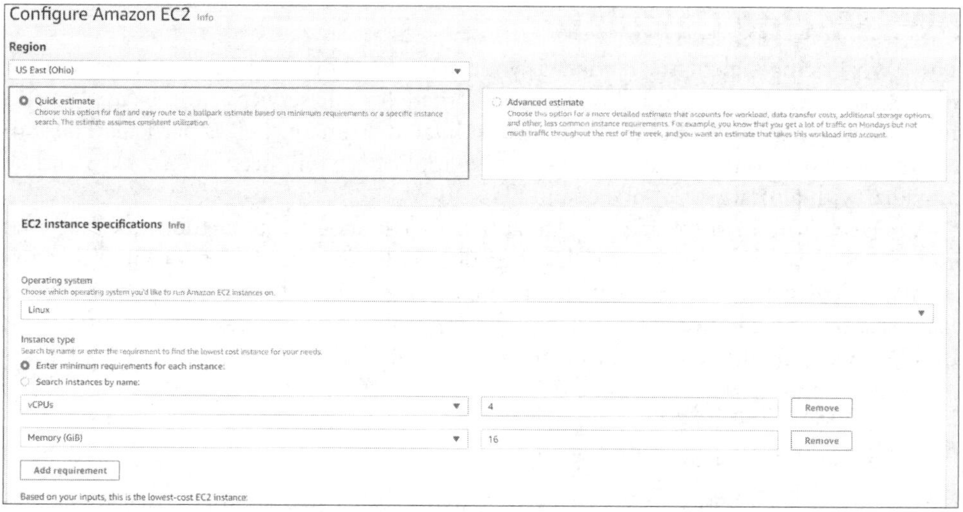

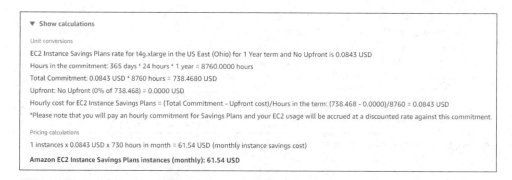

Figure 5-9 The AWS Pricing Calculator options under EC2 for Quick Estimate or Advanced Estimate

A powerful feature is the ability to create quotes for multiple services and resources to gain a full picture of estimated costs. This is useful for applications that will span multiple different provisions of a single service or those that span across multiple services. Building upon the simple example we used earlier for S3, we can also add an EC2 instance to our estimate using the following criteria, as shown calculated in Figure 5-10:

- Quick estimate
- Operating system: Linux
- vCPUs: 4
- Memory: 16GB
- EC2 instance type: t4g.xlarge
- EBS: 100GB gp2 storage

Show calculations
Unit conversions
EC2 Instance Savings Plans rate for t4g.xlarge in the US East (Ohio) for 1 Year term and No Upfront is 0.0843 USD
Hours in the commitment: 365 days * 24 hours * 1 year = 8760.0000 hours
Total Commitment: 0.0843 USD * 8760 hours = 738.4680 USD
Upfront: No Upfront (0% of 738.468) = 0.0000 USD
Hourly cost for EC2 Instance Savings Plans = (Total Commitment - Upfront cost)/Hours in the term: (738.468 - 0.0000)/8760 = 0.0843 USD
*Please note that you will pay an hourly commitment for Savings Plans and your EC2 usage will be accrued at a discounted rate against this commitment.
Pricing calculations
1 instances x 0.0843 USD x 730 hours in month = 61.54 USD (monthly instance savings cost)
Amazon EC2 Instance Savings Plans instances (monthly): 61.54 USD

Figure 5-10 Example calculations for a simple t4g.xlarge EC2 instance

Figure 5-11 Combined estimate including S3 and EC2 services

Once the calculations for both the S3 estimate and the EC2 estimate are combined, the Pricing Calculator will give a total estimate for all services, as shown in Figure 5-11.

On the same menu showing the combined billing estimate, you also have the option to add support to your services by utilizing the Add Support button on the upper right. This will add in support costs and be included in your overall estimate for services. Options are also available to save your estimate or export to a CSV.

Groups

A method that AWS provides for organizing estimates is through the use of groups. Groups can be used in many different ways to divide up resources based on your needs. They can be used to organize services by departments, cost centers, projects, or any other type of division that meets the criteria for why you need to generate estimates. By grouping services, you can store packages of services and then use overall estimates for easy comparison between varying degrees of resources or types of services. By generating estimates with multiple groups, you can arrive at a total cost of a project or system in AWS while still maintaining granularity to break down the estimate into specific components.

NOTE Due to pricing from the calculator being dependent upon AWS regions, a group is created specific to a region. If you need to obtain estimates for different or multiple regions, you will need to create a group for each one that contains your required services.

AWS Service Quotas

In order to protect the availability for all users in AWS, service quotas (formerly called limits) are applied to each service. These quotas are specific to a region and will place a limit on the number of specific types of resources you can allocate by default. For example, each type of EC2 instance would have a specific limit, such as 20, that can be allocated within that region. If you attempt to allocate more than this limit, the system will not allow you to submit the request.

While these service quotas are applied by default, the vast majority of them are capable of being increased by AWS should your needs require them. However, requesting an increase in a quota is a manual process, submitted via the Management Console, and must be processed by AWS. This means you will not get an immediate response to your request. You can view your quotas and submit requests for increases from the Service Quotas console, found at https://console.aws.amazon.com/servicequotas/home.

 NOTE You may be wondering why quotas exist at all if they can simply be increased at any time when such a request is made. Why are they set to a specific value? There are two reasons why they are used. The first is to serve as a guardrail against runaway costs and bills. The second, in some instances, is a technical limitation to preserve overall resources of the environment. Some technical limitations can still be increased, but they will still have an upper limit at some point that cannot be increased.

Once you log into your account, you will be presented with a dashboard that shows a default selection of AWS services, the total number of quotas applied to it, and any pending or recently resolved increase requests, as shown in Figure 5-12.

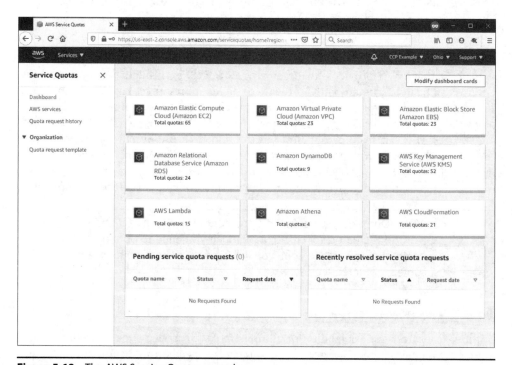

Figure 5-12 The AWS Service Quotas console

Amazon Simple Storage Service (Amazon S3)

Service quotas

[Request quota increase]

Q Filter by...   < 1 > ⚙

	Service quota ▲	Applied quota value	AWS default quota value	Adjustable ▽
○	Access Points	Not available	1,000	Yes
●	Bucket policy	Not available	20 Kilobytes	No
●	Bucket tags	Not available	50	No
○	Buckets	Not available	100	Yes
●	CRR rules	Not available	1,000	No
●	Event notifications	Not available	100	No
●	Lifecycle rules	Not available	1,000	No
●	Maximum part size	Not available	5 Gigabytes	No
●	Minimum part size	Not available	5 Megabytes	No
●	Object size	Not available	5 Terabytes	No
●	Object size (Console upload)	Not available	160 Gigabytes	No
●	Object tags	Not available	10	No
●	Parts	Not available	10,000	No
○	Replication transfer rate	Not available	1 Gigabits / Second	Yes
●	S3 Glacier: Number of random restore requests.	Not available	35	No
●	S3 Glacier: Provisioned capacity units	Not available	2	No

Figure 5-13   The S3 service quotas page

To illustrate the type of quotas that you may see for a service, going in to the S3 service will present you with a list of established quotas. These quotas range from the number of buckets you can create, maximum object size, and the number of S3 Glacier restore requests. A typical list of quotas for a service, in this case S3, is shown in Figure 5-13.

Selecting the "buckets" quota, you will see a menu that displays your current quota, your current usage, whether you can request an increase, and the specific URN (unique reference number) to your quota, as shown in Figure 5-14.

EXAM TIP   Remember that quotas are applied per region for each item. In the example for the S3 buckets, you will notice the URN for the quota is arn:aws:servicequotas:us-east-2::s3/L-DC2B2D3D, which signifies that it is in the us-east-2 region. Changing the region in the upper right to another will give you a different URN for that region, as well as different usage values.

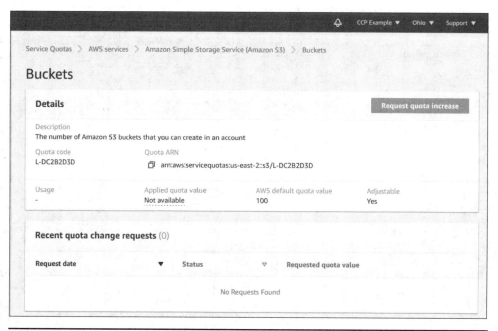

Figure 5-14 The S3 buckets quota dashboard

Reserved Instances

AWS allows users to pre-purchase resources and capacity for AWS EC2 services. These are based upon a one- or three-year commitment and can offer up to a 72 percent discount against the prices you would normally be charged when resources are allocated on-demand.

Reserve instances can be either standard or convertible:

- **Standard Reserve Instances** Offer up to 72 percent savings compared to on-demand pricing.

- **Convertible Reserve Instances** Offer up to 54 percent savings compared to on-demand pricing, but offer the ability to change the attributes later, as long as the new attributes are equal to or greater than the original reserve instance.

Reserved instances are based upon specific regions or Availability Zones and match specific criteria, such as instance type and specific resources. When you allocate a resource that matches the reserved instance, either manually or through automation, you will utilize those instances you have already purchased at the discounted rate. Figure 5-15 shows an example of savings for an a1.medium EC2 instance in the US East region.

EXAM TIP Make sure you understand the difference between standard and convertible reserve instances and how the savings and usage differ between them.

| Region: | US East (Ohio) ÷ | | | | | |

a1.medium

STANDARD 1-YEAR TERM						
Payment Option	Upfront	Monthly*	Effective Hourly**	Savings over On-Demand	On-Demand Hourly
No Upfront	$0	$11.75	$0.016	37%	
Partial Upfront	$67	$5.62	$0.015	40%	$0.0255
All Upfront	$131	$0.00	$0.015	41%	

CONVERTIBLE 1-YEAR TERM						
Payment Option	Upfront	Monthly*	Effective Hourly**	Savings over On-Demand	On-Demand Hourly
No Upfront	$0	$13.51	$0.019	27%	
Partial Upfront	$77	$6.42	$0.018	31%	$0.0255
All Upfront	$151	$0.00	$0.017	32%	

STANDARD 3-YEAR TERM						
Payment Option	Upfront	Monthly*	Effective Hourly**	Savings over On-Demand	On-Demand Hourly
No Upfront	$0	$8.03	$0.011	57%	
Partial Upfront	$134	$3.72	$0.010	60%	$0.0255
All Upfront	$252	$0.00	$0.010	62%	

Figure 5-15 AWS reserve instance savings example, based on the a1.medium instance type in the US East region

Savings Plans

Savings plans are a pricing model for AWS compute usage that offers up to a 72 percent discount on on-demand pricing by committing to purchasing a set amount of compute power (in $/hour) over a one- or three-year span, similar to reserved instances. Savings plans apply across instance types, size, operation system, or region and also apply to the AWS Fargate and Lambda services.

There are two types of savings plans:

- **Compute Savings Plans**   Offer up to a 66 percent discount on on-demand pricing to be used across the compute services of EC2, Lambda, and Fargate
- **EC2 Instance Savings Plans**   Offer up to a 72 percent discount on on-demand pricing but apply to specific instance types in specific regions

Pricing for savings plans can be found at https://aws.amazon.com/savingsplans/pricing/.

AWS Billing Dashboard

The AWS Billing Dashboard provides you all the tools you need to view your bills, monitor your usage and costs, and set up consolidated billing for multiple accounts. You can access your AWS Billing Dashboard at https://console.aws.amazon.com/billing.

The Billing Dashboard contains direct links down the left side to all of the functions that are necessary to manage your account, as shown in Figure 5-16.

Viewing Your Bill

From within the Billing Dashboard, you can access your bill by clicking on the Bills link on the left side. This will take you into your bills, and you can use the dropdown at the top to change between months.

Each bill will be itemized for all of the services that you have used during the month. This will also include anything you have used in the Free Tier, but with a $0 cost associated with it. The example bill shown in Figure 5-17 includes the example services from earlier exercises, such as S3 bucket creation and usage of the AWS Key Management Service.

TIP At the top of the bill in the right corner you will see options to print or download the bill in CSV. If you only have a small number of services like we have used in the exercises, it is easy to see on the dashboard, but the more services you provision, the more useful downloading via CSV will be. The downloaded CSV can also be used to import into accounting, payment, or reporting systems that your organization may use.

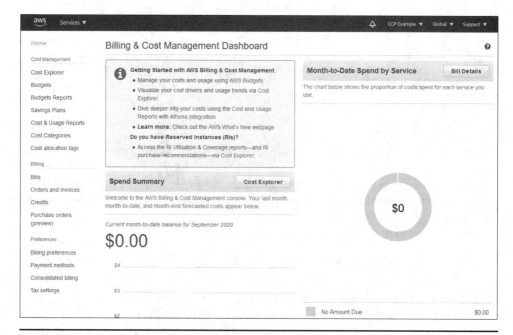

Figure 5-16 The AWS Billing & Cost Management Dashboard

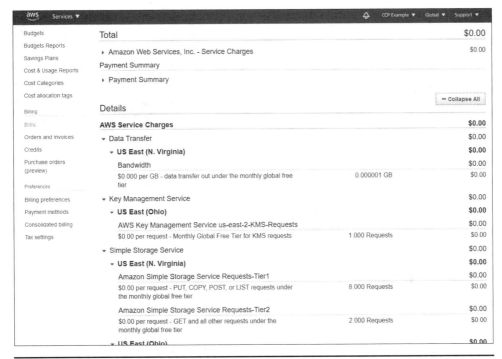

Figure 5-17 A sample AWS monthly bill showing usage of services in the Free Tier

Monitoring Your Usage and Costs

With the pricing model based on charges incurred for services used, and only for the time when they are being used, the ability to monitor both your usage and costs is very important. AWS provides several tools on the Billing Dashboard to assist with both aspects.

Cost Explorer

Cost Explorer allows you to view and analyze both your costs and usage of AWS services. Cost Explorer will display data for 12 months of usage, as well as provide forecasts for what you may use in the next 12 months based on your past usage.

Cost Explorer provides several reconfigured views that will get you started with an overview of your costs and usage and provide a framework for customizations you may desire for your specific needs. The first time you launch Cost Explorer, it will take up to 24 hours to prepare data from your last 12 months and process the forecasts for the next 12 months. It will also walk you through the sections and explain what each is used for the first time you use it.

You can filter reports in Cost Explorer in many customizable ways, such as by date, region, Availability Zone, platforms, instance types, etc. You can save reports for future usage and can download any reports in CSV format as well.

Cost Explorer is provided free to AWS users and will update reports at least once every 24 hours ongoing.

AWS Budgets

Budgets are used to plan the consumption of services, costs of services, and the use of instance reservations. They can be used to track how close you are to using a budgeted amount of money, as well as the use of the Free Tier. This also includes your usage during a specified time period, including your usage of reservation instances, as well as how much of your overall budget has been used. During each month, budgets will track how much your current charged status is, including what your predicted amount of usage and charges will be by the end of the month.

Budgets are updated on a regular basis, typically every 8 to 12 hours, up to three times per day. You can create a variety of different types of budgets to suit your needs, and each account can create up 20,000 budgets!

- **Cost budgets**   Allow for planning what your ceiling will be for spending on a particular service.

- **Usage budgets**   Allow you to plan how much actual usage of a particular service you want to use.

- **Reserved instances budgets**   Track your usage of reserved instances to determine if they are unused or if you have purchased too much. These also allow for alerts to be received when your number of reserved instances falls below specific thresholds.

- **Reserved instances coverage budgets**   Track how much of your resource allocations and service usage is covered by your reserved instances.

- **Savings plans utilization budgets**   Track usage of savings plans based on utilization and trigger alerts when falling under the thresholds.

- **Savings plans coverage budgets**   Track and alert when your usage of savings plans falls under a threshold.

NOTE   Due to budgets being updated every 8 to 12 hours, it is possible for your services and costs to exceed your budget during those periods between updates. Keep in mind that budgets only act as a reporting and alerting service. They will not stop or contain your services.

Budget Reports

By using AWS Budgets, you can create reports to be generated on a daily, weekly, or monthly frequency. Each budget report generated can be e-mailed to up to 50 e-mail addresses, and each report will cost $0.01. This cost is regardless of what kind of budget report is generated—it is a flat cost per report and does not change based on the number of recipients.

Detecting Unusual Spending

Anomaly detection is a new machine learning service that monitors your account on a continuous basis to detect unusual amounts of spending. The service will send individual reports when an anomaly is detected and will analyze the cause of the anomaly to isolate it to an account, region, or type of usage. Through the use of machine learning, over time false positives can be minimized as more data on your typical usage and peak periods is logged. The service allows for analysis to be grouped by AWS service, accounts, cost allocation tags, or cost categories.

Cost Categories

Cost categories allow an account to categorize services and costs into granular containers for the purposes of analysis based on your specific needs. Services can be grouped into categories based on projects, departments, initiatives, or any other category that is tracked and important to a user. This also allows services to appear in multiple cost categories. For example, you may decide to create a category for each team or division and the services that are part of their budget or responsibility. This will give you an organizational view of costs in a typical structure. You can also opt to create categories than span organizational charts along the lines of services or initiatives, such as a new product launch or special projects, and determine specific costs related to them from a more overview level. This can also be very useful with contractors and service companies, where teams and divisions may span multiple accounts and can categorize costs at the level of the specific team but also realize costs for each different account that those teams work on.

Cost Allocation Tags

Cost allocation tags are metadata assigned to AWS resources in the form of a key and a value. These can be used to allow an account to quickly track costs associated with resources through very granular views. Cost allocation tags are either generated automatically by AWS or are created by users. The AWS tags will contain information of a system nature, such as created dates, created by what user, region, etc. User tags are defined by the user based on their organization and can include items like project, stack, team, cost center, etc.

For example, an EC2 instance might contain the following metadata in Table 5-1 attached to it.

By defining tags on services, reports can be generated on any specific tag. This will allow users to quickly analyze costs based on any of their tags such as stack, project, or cost center, or even use AWS-generated tags to track by creation date or user. In order to use cost allocation tags, they must each be activated from the Billing Dashboard. You can opt to activate either the AWS-generated tags or the user tags, or both. Once they are activated, they will appear in Cost Explorer and can be used in reporting.

Table 5-1
Example Key/
Value Pairs of Cost
Allocation Tags

Key	Value
aws:createdDate	20200901
user:Cost Center	5648716
user:Project	Marketing
user:Stack	Production

Consolidated Billing

If you have multiple accounts in AWS, you can opt to consolidate your billing into a single monthly bill, rather than receiving separate bills for each account. With consolidated billing, even though you will only receive one bill, it will still be broken down by individual accounts for tracking purposes and auditing. The great benefit of consolidated billing is the ability to share volume discounts, reserved instance discounts, and savings plans across all of your accounts, rather than each account having its own. This can lead to considerable costs savings across an organization. Consolidated billing is free to AWS users.

 NOTE Whole consolidated billing allows you to leverage discounts across multiple accounts, but support plans are still billed on an individual account basis. The costs of support plans will show up in a consolidated bill with an aggregate amount, but the costs are independently calculated from each account.

Billing Security

Just as AWS is responsible for securing all of their services, they also provide robust security for billing and customer financial data. The same rigorous security mechanisms that are applied to their services, including auditing and logging, is also applied to activities within the Billing Dashboard. This also means that you must protect your billing data with the same rigor as you would other institutional and user data and ensure that you are complying with any regulatory requirements that are applicable to financial and accounting data for your jurisdiction.

Billing Support

AWS provides support for billing through their normal channels of technical and security services. This includes the Knowledge Center and official AWS support through tickets opened through your Management Console and the AWS Support Center. You can also use AWS forums to seek assistance with managing your costs and estimates.

 NOTE When using a support option such as forums, be very careful to not divulge any actual financial or billing information when you ask questions or assist others.

AWS IQ

If you need assistance with compiling estimates for AWS services or assistance with determining what you actually need, another resource that is available is the AWS IQ service, which offers AWS Certified freelancers and consulting firms. Information about the AWS IQ service can be found at https://iq.aws.amazon.com/.

Exercise 5-1: Generate a Pricing Estimate for VPN Through VPC

1. Go to the AWS Price Calculator at https://calculator.aws/.

2. Click on the Create Estimate button.

3. Type **VPC** in the search box, and then click the Configure button within the box for Amazon Virtual Private Cloud (VPC).

4. Select options to match what is shown in the following illustration:

   a. Select the US East (Ohio) region from the dropdown.

   b. Select VPN Connection.

   c. Enter **20** for the Number of Site-to-Site VPN Connections.

   d. Enter **24** and **hours per day** for the Average Duration For Each Connection.

   e. Click Add To My Estimate at the bottom-right corner.

5. You will now receive an estimate, shown next, calculating the costs of the service you just estimated, including total up-front costs, total monthly costs, and the total for the first 12 months.

6. Keep this browser window open, as we will use the work you have already done in the next exercise

---

Exercise 5-2: Generate a Pricing Estimate for Multiple Services

1. With the estimate you already made in Exercise 5-1, click on the Add Service button on the top-right corner.

2. Type **EC2** in the search box, and then click on the Configure button within the Amazon EC2 box.

3. Select the options to match what is shown in the following illustration. Note that the system has automatically selected the r5a.xlarge instance type based on the options selected.

   a. Quick estimate

   b. Operating system: Windows Server

   c. vCPUs: 4

   d. Memory (GiB): 32

e. Quantity: 1

f. Scroll to the bottom and click Add To My Estimate.

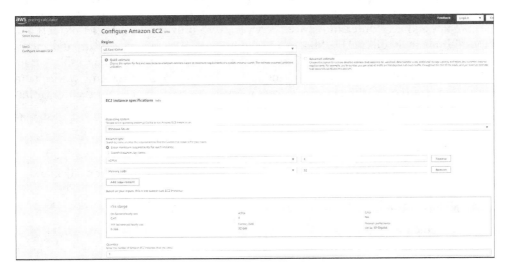

4. You will now receive an estimate, shown next, calculating the costs of both services you just estimated, including total up-front costs, total monthly costs, and the total for the first 12 months.

5. Feel free to continue to add services or support to get a feel for how the calculator works and the various options that are available for each service.

Chapter Review

In this chapter we explored the various pricing models that AWS uses across their services. With the enormous complexity and diversity of AWS services, pricing models can be complex and very different between services. AWS provides a robust set of tools and reports from their Billing Dashboard to empower users to estimate, plan, and monitor costs, as well as reporting on costs when thresholds are approaching limits or are exceeded. AWS billing tools offer enormous flexibility to users for tracking services and costs from a variety of different approaches to meet the specific needs of their organization or services.

Questions

1. Which type of reserve instance receives the largest cost savings over on-demand pricing?

   A. Enterprise

   B. Standard

   C. Convertible

   D. Aggregated

2. How many recipients can you send budget reports to?

   A. 100

   B. 50

   C. 10

   D. 1

3. How many budgets may be created within an AWS account?

   A. 10,000

   B. 1,000 per service

   C. 20,000

   D. Unlimited

4. What are the two types of cost allocation tags that are available to use for cost and budget tracking? (Select two.)

   A. AWS

   B. Service

   C. User

   D. Account

5. At what level are AWS service quotas applied?

    A. Availability Zone

    B. VPC

    C. Account

    D. Region

6. Which of the following is not a category of free offerings within the AWS Free Tier?

    A. Always

    B. Preview

    C. 12 months

    D. Trials

7. Which AWS service does not apply across accounts through the use of consolidated billing?

    A. Volume discounts

    B. Reserved instances

    C. Savings plans

    D. Support

8. Which of the following frequencies of reports is not offered by the budget reports service?

    A. Yearly

    B. Daily

    C. Weekly

    D. Monthly

9. What service connects AWS users with AWS Certified freelancers or consulting firms?

    A. AWS Consulting

    B. AWS IQ

    C. AWS Independent Services

    D. AWS Professional Services

10. What data format is supported for exporting your bill?

    A. XML

    B. JSON

    C. CSV

    D. PDF

Questions and Answers

1. Which type of reserve instance receives the largest cost savings over on-demand pricing?

   A. Enterprise

   B. Standard

   C. Convertible

   D. Aggregated

   ☑ **B.** Standard reserve instances receive up to a 72 percent savings over on-demand pricing but must be used for the same time of the instance they were purchased for.

2. How many recipients can you send budget reports to?

   A. 100

   B. 50

   C. 10

   D. 1

   ☑ **B.** Budget reports may be sent to up to 50 e-mail addresses.

3. How many budgets may be created within an AWS account?

   A. 10,000

   B. 1,000 per service

   C. 20,000

   D. Unlimited

   ☑ **C.** Each AWS account may create up to 20,000 budgets.

4. What are the two types of cost allocation tags that are available to use for cost and budget tracking? (Select two.)

   A. AWS

   B. Service

   C. User

   D. Account

   ☑ **A, C.** Cost allocation tags are either AWS generated or user generated. Each must be activated separately before used in Cost Explorer.

5. At what level are AWS service quotas applied?

   A. Availability Zone

   B. VPC

   C. Account

   D. Region

    ☑ **D.** AWS service quotas are applied at the region level and are independent across the regions.

6. Which of the following is not a category of free offerings within the AWS Free Tier?

   A. Always

   B. Preview

   C. 12 months

   D. Trials

    ☑ **B.** Preview is not a category of free offerings from the AWS Free Tier. The categories are Always, 12 months, and Trials.

7. Which AWS service does not apply across accounts through the use of consolidated billing?

   A. Volume discounts

   B. Reserved instances

   C. Savings plans

   D. Support

    ☑ **D.** Support costs are applied at the individual account level. While they will appear with an aggregate total on consolidated bills, they are shared between accounts, and each account must purchase them separately.

8. Which of the following frequencies of reports is not offered by the budget reports service?

   A. Yearly

   B. Daily

   C. Weekly

   D. Monthly

    ☑ **A.** Budget reports are available daily, weekly, or monthly; yearly is not an option.

9. What service connects AWS users with AWS Certified freelancers or consulting firms?

   A. AWS Consulting

   B. AWS IQ

   C. AWS Independent Services

   D. AWS Professional Services

   ☑ **B.** The AWS IQ service connects users with AWS Certified freelancers and consulting firms.

10. What data format is supported for exporting your bill?

   A. XML

   B. JSON

   C. CSV

   D. PDF

   ☑ **C.** You are able to export your AWS Bill into the CSV format.

Objective Map

Exam CLF-C01

Official Exam Objective	Chapter No.
1.0 Cloud Concepts	
1.1 Define the AWS Cloud and its value proposition	2
1.2 Identify aspects of AWS Cloud economics	2
1.3 List the different cloud architecture design principles	2
2.0 Security and Compliance	
2.1 Define the AWS shared responsibility model	3
2.2 Define AWS Cloud security and compliance concepts	3
2.3 Identify AWS access management capabilities	3
2.4 Identify resources for security support	3
3.0 Technology	
3.1 Define methods of deploying and operating in the AWS Cloud	4
3.2 Define the AWS global infrastructure	4
3.3 Identify the core AWS services	4
3.4 Identify resources for technology support	4
4.0 Billing and Pricing	
4.1 Compare and contrast the various pricing models for AWS	5
4.2 Recognize the various account structures in relation to AWS billing and pricing	5
4.3 Identify resources available for billing support	5

AWS Certified Cloud Practitioner Practice Exam

The following is a full-length practice exam of the AWS CCP. This contains 65 questions, the same as the actual exam, and is weighted to draw questions from the domains with the same percentage as the actual exam.

You should set up a 90-minute window of time to try this exam to replicate what the actual exam will be like. Following the questions are correct answer explanations.

Questions

1. Your company has decided to use AWS S3 to store archived data that is required for regulatory compliance but is not accessed otherwise. However, when it is required, it must be produced within 24 hours. Which S3 storage type would be the most cost-effective choice to meet these requirements?

   A. S3 One Zone-Infrequent Access

   B. S3 Glacier

   C. S3 Standard-Infrequent Access

   D. S3 Glacier Deep

2. In order to use the AWS CLI, what is required, regardless of the platform you are using to originate your CLI commands? (Choose two.)

   A. Outbound access on port 443

   B. Access/secret key

   C. Root user credentials

   D. MFA

   E. AWS access gateway

3. You have an enterprise support plan in AWS and have an upcoming disaster recovery drill that you need AWS involvement in. Which AWS support resource would you reach out to for this?

   A. AWS technical account manager

   B. AWS Professional Services

   C. AWS DR engineers

   D. AWS consulting services

4. When versioning is enabled within the S3 service, at what level is it controlled?

   A. Region

   B. Object

   C. Bucket

   D. Availability Zone

5. Amazon Aurora is a database service that incorporates two popular databases that are widely used by software packages. Which two databases are part of Aurora?

   A. Microsoft SQL Server

   B. Oracle

   C. MySQL

   D. MariaDB

   E. PostgreSQL

6. The AWS Free Tier has three different categories of free services. Which of the following is not a category of the Free Tier?

   A. Trials

   B. Always free

   C. 12-months free

   D. Free scaling

7. You need to store data objects in S3 that will be infrequently requested, but when they are requested, you need to have immediate response and high availability. Which S3 storage class would be the most cost-effective to use for this requirement?

   A. S3 Standard

   B. S3 Standard-Infrequent Access

   C. S3 Intelligent-Tiering

   D. S3 One Zone-Infrequent Access

8. Under the developer service plan, you receive different guarantees of support time response for both general guidance issues and system problems. Which combination of response times is associated with the developer support plan?

   A. 24 hours for general guidance, 12 hours for system problems

   B. 48 hours for general guidance, 24 hours for system problems

   C. 12 hours for general guidance, 6 hours for system problems

   D. 12 hours for general guidance, 1 hour for system problems

9. AWS Edge allows for ultra-low-latency access to data through a network of locations throughout the world and specializing in a few services. Which of the following AWS services use Edge? (Choose two.)

   A. Lightsail

   B. DynamoDB

   C. AWS Storage Gateway

   D. CloudFront

   E. Route 53

10. Which AWS service would be considered an Infrastructure as a Service offering?

   A. Lightsail

   B. AppStream

   C. EC2

   D. Elastic Beanstalk

11. In order to add resources to your system, there is a cost in the form of required downtime or starts to services. With this assumption, what is your system said to be?

   A. Scalable

   B. Elastic

   C. Expandable

   D. Redundant

12. Your data center has become unreliable and slow in terms of Internet connectivity due to a natural disaster. You have decided it is time to move all data into AWS and retire your data center to prevent this problem from happening again. With the problems of unreliability and slowness, which AWS service would facilitate moving this large amount of data into AWS?

   A. AWS Snowcone

   B. AWS Snowmobile

   C. AWS Snowball

   D. AWS Snowplow

13. What is the minimum duration of usage of an AWS service for billing purposes?

    A. One month

    B. One day

    C. No minimum

    D. One billing cycle

14. Which AWS service would be used by developers for packaging deployment packages for application code?

    A. CodeCommit

    B. CodeDeploy

    C. CodeBuild

    D. CodeCompile

15. What types of reserved instances are available on AWS? (Choose two.)

    A. Standard

    B. Conforming

    C. Scalable

    D. Convertible

    E. Flexible

16. Which AWS service allows you to purchase reserved instances?

    A. S3

    B. EC2

    C. Lightsail

    D. CloudWatch

17. Route 53 can dynamically return different answers to DNS queries based on different circumstances within the AWS infrastructure. Which of the following are circumstances that can be configured with Route 53 to give dynamic responses? (Choose two.)

    A. Geographic location

    B. Incoming port

    C. Latency of systems

    D. Size of transfer request

    E. ACL rules

18. Three types of load balancing are used under Elastic Load Balancing. Which of the following is not one of the three types?

    A. Application load balancer

    B. Network load balancer

    C. Dynamic load balancer

    D. Classic load balancer

19. As part of an external audit, you need to provide a list of all users and the access they have within your AWS account. Which report from the IAM console would you generate to provide the auditors this information?

    A. Credential report

    B. User report

    C. IAM report

    D. Account audit report

20. Which of the following statements best describes Software as a Service?

    A. The cloud customer is responsible for deploying and configuring virtual machines based upon a managed image.

    B. The cloud customer gets access to a fully managed service via subscription versus installed locally.

    C. The cloud customer gives the user a fully managed platform where only the specific software needed by the user is loaded.

    D. The cloud provider establishes a network and virtualization infrastructure where virtual machines are loaded as software for users to configure.

21. The data your application hosts has strict regulatory requirements that you must meet. Which component of the AWS infrastructure would you be most focused on when deploying resources?

    A. Availability Zones

    B. Regions

    C. Edge services

    D. VPC

22. Which of the following technologies would be used as a security protection for data in transit?

    A. VPC

    B. VPN

    C. ACLs

    D. Security groups

    E. TLS

23. When looking at the AWS Management Console, you are not seeing services that you have provisioned. Which of the following could be a reason why?

  A. You have not paid for them

  B. Your account requires new access keys

  C. You have not selected the correct region

  D. The console does not show reserved instances

24. You have a rule in a security group that allows HTTPS requests into an EC2 instance. Which statement is true about how the security policy applies to responses to the request?

  A. The response will be blocked without a corresponding rule allowing it

  B. A corresponding ACL must be present to allow the response

  C. Security groups automatically have the same rules for inbound and outbound requests

  D. Security groups will automatically allow traffic that is a response to an allowed request, regardless of what the rules specify

25. Savings plans on AWS offer deep discounts over on-demand pricing based on a commitment for future purchase. Which service is not covered by savings plans?

  A. S3

  B. EC2

  C. Lambda

  D. Fargate

26. The AWS monthly billing allows for the export and downloading of data. Which format is offered to download your billing data?

  A. JSON

  B. XML

  C. QuickBooks

  D. CSV

27. AWS Budgets offers a variety of different planning templates to help users track service consumption and charges. Which of the following are types of budget reports offered? (Choose two.)

  A. Usage budgets

  B. Overage budgets

  C. Storage budgets

  D. Savings plans coverage budgets

  E. Virtualization budgets

28. You need to be able to quickly verify if data objects in AWS are identical across multiple regions in S3. Which type of algorithm would allow you to quickly and easily accomplish this?

   A. Tokenization

   B. Hashing

   C. Obfuscation

   D. Encryption

29. You want to run a dynamic website in AWS but do not want to be responsible for deploying or maintaining any servers or software beyond your own application code. Which of the following AWS services would allow you to accomplish this? (Choose two.)

   A. Lightsail

   B. Lambda

   C. CloudFront

   D. CloudTrail

   E. EC2

30. AWS OpsWorks provides managed instances of popular automation and configuration tools. Which popular utilities are available within OpsWorks? (Choose two.)

   A. Git

   B. SVN

   C. Puppet

   D. CVS

   E. Chef

31. AWS offers the ability to download or export many reports within the Management Console that you can then use for local processing or importing into other tools. Which data format is offered to export the data from the Management Console?

   A. CSV

   B. JSON

   C. XML

   D. SQL

32. You suspect one of your employees has been violating company policy with the use of AWS services under your account for personal use. Which AWS service would be valuable to investigate their activities?

   A. CloudTrail

   B. CloudWatch

   C. CloudAudit

   D. CloudLog

33. Rather than using your on-premises VDI solutions, which AWS service could be leveraged to provide your users the same functionality while removing your need to maintain and support a hardware infrastructure?

A. AppStream

B. WorkSpaces

C. WorkLink

D. AWS DaaS

34. Your company wants to split budgets out in multiple ways in order to gain insight into costs by department and projects. Which AWS tool under the Billing Dashboard will allow easy implementation of this?

A. Cost centers

B. Cost graphs

C. Cost categories

D. Cost codes

35. AWS incorporates a variety of robust security services to counter common types of web attacks. Which type of attack is the AWS Shield service designed to protect against?

A. Cross-site scripting

B. SQL injection

C. Brute force

D. Distributed Denial of Service

36. You need to provide application access to a subset of users to test and verify functionality but do not want them to see production data. What type of data deidentification process would you use for this?

A. Static masking

B. Dynamic masking

C. PII masking

D. Sensitivity masking

37. What is the easiest method to implement encryption at rest within S3 from the perspective of the user?

A. Client-side encryption using keys generated by AWS

B. Server-side encryption using your own keys

C. Server-side encryption using keys generated by AWS

D. Client-side encryption using your own keys

38. With consolidated billing you can merge multiple accounts into a single bill and leverage the combined resources for discounts on AWS services. Which of the following is not a cost that receives discounts under consolidated billing?

   A. EC2

   B. Support plans

   C. Lambda

   D. Fargate

39. The AWS Marketplace offers images from vendors that are full packages for their products that can be deployed within AWS. Costs for Marketplace offerings have two components. Which of the following are the price components? (Choose two.)

   A. S3 costs

   B. EC2 costs

   C. Support costs

   D. Licensing costs

   E. Professional services costs

40. Your company has decided to retire their on-premises data warehouse and move to a similar solution in AWS for increased capacity and lower costs. Which AWS service would you explore for this initiative?

   A. Redshift

   B. Aurora

   C. DynamoDB

   D. RDS

41. Which type of service offerings pushes the responsibility for configuration and operations to AWS and leaves the customer only responsible for loading their data?

   A. Unmanaged

   B. Regulated

   C. Managed

   D. Offloaded

42. When users are created via the IAM console, what can be used to assign granular levels of access within a service?

   A. Groups

   B. Roles

   C. ACLs

   D. Settings

43. A system is able to keep functioning when some portions of it experience an outage of resources. What concept refers to this ability?

   A. Availability

   B. Resiliency

   C. Redundancy

   D. Elasticity

44. AWS allows for resources to be added to a system without any downtime or interruption to services. What is this concept called?

   A. Elasticity

   B. Scalability

   C. Expandability

   D. Portability

45. Which component of AWS Systems Manager provides a consolidated view of data from sources such as CloudTrail and CloudWatch to help with the investigation of operational issues?

   A. Explorer

   B. AppConfig

   C. Systems Manager

   D. OpsCenter

46. Security groups and access control lists (ACLs) are two means of applying security rules within AWS. Which of the following statements is true?

   A. Security groups and ACLs can both be applied to subnets and instances

   B. Security groups apply to instances; ACLs apply to subnets

   C. Security groups apply to subnets; ACLs apply to instances

   D. Security groups and ACLs are only used on subnets

47. To help manage versioning in AWS S3, the service provides automation tools, called actions, to handle how versions are stored and when they are removed from the system. Which of the following are the types of actions available? (Choose two.)

   A. Archive

   B. Transition

   C. Delete

   D. Rotate

   E. Expire

48. Under the AWS Shared Responsibility Model and an IaaS implementation, which of the following areas of responsibility reside with the customer? (Choose two.)

  A. Application code

  B. Operating system

  C. Virtualization

  D. Storage

  E. Networking

49. The use of multifactor authentication is imperative to protect accounts with administrative access, especially the root user for your AWS account. Along with a password, which of the following could be used to fulfill multifactor requirements?

  A. PIN

  B. Question/answer challenge

  C. One-time use code

  D. Date of birth

50. Rather than creating accounts with passwords in AWS, your corporate policies require you to use your internal credentials via federation with AWS. Which technology could you use to establish federated authentication with AWS?

  A. JSON

  B. HTTPS

  C. RADIUS

  D. SAML

51. When adding new users in IAM, you want to be able to assign a set of capabilities to them and keep them uniform between those users. Which feature of IAM would you use to accomplish this?

  A. Groups

  B. Labels

  C. Roles

  D. Sets

52. Which core concept of cloud computing most relates to the cost-savings benefits you can realize through AWS offerings?

  A. Broad network access

  B. On-demand self-service

  C. Metered service

  D. Resource pooling

53. Which AWS support plan is the lowest level that gives 24/7 access to support?

    A. Free

    B. Business

    C. Enterprise

    D. Developer

54. Your company has decided for the first time to start using AWS services for storage. As a precondition, your CEO has demanded assurances that you can quickly remove data from AWS should the need arise. Which core concept of cloud computing would this pertain to?

    A. Portability

    B. Reversibility

    C. Interoperability

    D. Removability

55. The Trust Advisor can flag AWS services that you have provisioned but are inactive or being used below the level for which they are configured. Which area of Trust Advisor would you explore to find this report?

    A. Performance

    B. Service limits

    C. Cost optimization

    D. Security

56. You want to do a compliance check with your configurations against best practices. Which AWS service would you use to accomplish this?

    A. Trusted Advisor

    B. IAM dashboard

    C. AWS Management Console

    D. AWS System Manager

57. You need to offer easy access to your AWS systems from anywhere, but you do not want to deal with many of the problems of BYOD and the security issues associated with it. Which AWS service would you investigate to accomplish this?

    A. OpsWorks

    B. Lambda

    C. Aurora

    D. WorkSpaces

58. When using the AWS Virtual Private Cloud to span between AWS resources and your on-premises resources, what type of cloud deployment are you using?

    A. Public

    B. Community

    C. Private

    D. Hybrid

59. Which concept of cloud computing refers to the ability of a system to easily move between different cloud providers?

    A. Interoperability

    B. Portability

    C. Moveability

    D. Transferability

60. Which AWS database service does not use SQL and is highly optimized for key-value data storage?

    A. DynamoDB

    B. Aurora

    C. Redshift

    D. CloudFront

61. Which component of the AWS Management Console allows a user to access the shell and CLI for managing EC2 instances without the use of keys or exposing ports?

    A. Run command

    B. Distributor

    C. Systems Manager

    D. Automation

62. An academic institution has a suite of software packages that it wants to make available to students but does not want to distribute software or be responsible for the support of it on student devices. Which AWS service would be the easiest and most cost-effective means to accomplish this?

    A. WorkSpaces

    B. AppStream

    C. WorkLink

    D. VirtualApp

63. Which AWS security service would allow you to apply processing rules to web traffic based upon the contents or type of request?

  A. AWS Shield

  B. Route 53

  C. AWS WAF

  D. AWS Inspector

64. Which AWS storage service is used by EC2 instances for high-throughput data operations?

  A. S3

  B. AWS Storage Gateway

  C. Elastic Block Storage

  D. AWS Snow

65. You want to use a set of configurations within your code that will use the same key value on all systems but have different values based upon the specific system. Which AWS tool allows you to do this?

  A. Parameter store

  B. State manager

  C. Distributor

  D. Automation

Questions and Answers

1. Your company has decided to use AWS S3 to store archived data that is required for regulatory compliance but is not accessed otherwise. However, when it is required, it must be produced within 24 hours. Which S3 storage type would be the most cost-effective choice to meet these requirements?

  A. S3 One Zone-Infrequent Access

  B. S3 Glacier

  C. S3 Standard-Infrequent Access

  D. S3 Glacier Deep

  ☑ **D.** S3 Glacier Deep is the cheapest storage offering under S3 and can deliver on the requirements for 24-hour retrieval.

2. In order to use the AWS CLI, what is required, regardless of the platform you are using to originate your CLI commands? (Choose two.)

  A. Outbound access on port 443

  B. Access/secret key

   C. Root user credentials

   D. MFA

   E. AWS access gateway

   ☑ **A, B.** To use the AWS CLI, you will need outbound access via port 443 from your system to AWS, as well as an access/secret key from the IAM console.

3. You have an enterprise support plan in AWS and have an upcoming disaster recovery drill that you need AWS involvement in. Which AWS support resource would you reach out to for this?

   A. AWS technical account manager

   B. AWS Professional Services

   C. AWS DR engineers

   D. AWS consulting services

   ☑ **A.** The AWS Technical Account Manager will participate in disaster recovery planning and drills, as well as provide a personal and direct contact for any support or account issues.

4. When versioning is enabled within the S3 service, at what level is it controlled?

   A. Region

   B. Object

   C. Bucket

   D. Availability Zone

   ☑ **C.** Versioning can only be enabled at the bucket level and applies to all objects within the bucket. Once you have it enabled, when you upload a new copy of an object, S3 will preserve the previous copy.

5. Amazon Aurora is a database service that incorporates two popular databases that are widely used by software packages. Which two databases are part of Aurora?

   A. Microsoft SQL Server

   B. Oracle

   C. MySQL

   D. MariaDB

   E. PostgreSQL

   ☑ **C, E.** Aurora is an AWS database service, a subset of Amazon RDS, that is compatible with both MySQL and PostgreSQL databases. It combines the features and simplicity of the open-source databases with the robust management and security of AWS services.

6. The AWS Free Tier has three different categories of free services. Which of the following is not a category of the Free Tier?

   A. Trials

   B. Always free

   C. 12-months free

   D. Free scaling

   ☑ **D.** Free scaling is not one of the categories of the AWS Free Tier. The correct categories are Always free, 12-months free, and trials.

7. You need to store data objects in S3 that will be infrequently requested, but when they are requested, you need to have immediate response and high availability. Which S3 storage class would be the most cost-effective to use for this requirement?

   A. S3 Standard

   B. S3 Standard-Infrequent Access

   C. S3 Intelligent-Tiering

   D. S3 One Zone-Infrequent Access

   ☑ **B.** S3 Standard-Infrequent access would be the most cost-effective where immediate response and high availability were required. While S3 One Zone-Infrequent access would also give the immediate response required, it lacks the fault tolerance necessary for high availability.

8. Under the developer service plan, you receive different guarantees of support time response for both general guidance issues and system problems. Which combination of response times is associated with the developer support plan?

   A. 24 hours for general guidance, 12 hours for system problems

   B. 48 hours for general guidance, 24 hours for system problems

   C. 12 hours for general guidance, 6 hours for system problems

   D. 12 hours for general guidance, 1 hour for system problems

   ☑ **A.** The developer support plan promises less than 24 hours response time for general guidance questions and less than 12 hours response time for system problems and issues.

9. AWS Edge allows for ultra-low-latency access to data through a network of locations throughout the world and specializing in a few services. Which of the following AWS services use Edge? (Choose two.)

   A. Lightsail

   B. DynamoDB

   C. AWS Storage Gateway

D. CloudFront

E. Route 53

☑ **D, E.** The CloudFront Content Delivery Network, which stores cached copies of data close to users, and the Route 53 DNS service both use AWS Edge.

10. Which AWS service would be considered an Infrastructure as a Service offering?

A. Lightsail

B. AppStream

C. EC2

D. Elastic Beanstalk

☑ **C.** EC2 would be considered an IaaS offering, as the user is responsible for all configuration and maintenance of everything from the operating system and up.

11. In order to add resources to your system, there is a cost in the form of required downtime or starts to services. With this assumption, what is your system said to be?

A. Scalable

B. Elastic

C. Expandable

D. Redundant

☑ **A.** A system is considered scalable when resources can be added or removed from it, but with a required restart or downtime associated with the change.

12. Your data center has become unreliable and slow in terms of Internet connectivity due to a natural disaster. You have decided it is time to move all data into AWS and retire your data center to prevent this problem from happening again. With the problems of unreliability and slowness, which AWS service would facilitate moving this large amount of data into AWS?

A. AWS Snowcone

B. AWS Snowmobile

C. AWS Snowball

D. AWS Snowplow

☑ **B.** AWS Snowmobile is a 45-foot ruggedized shipping container that is outfitted with 100 petabytes of storage capacity. It is driven to the site of the customer and connected for data transfers. It is then transported to an AWS data center, connected to the network, and data is transferred into the Amazon S3 service.

13. What is the minimum duration of usage of an AWS service for billing purposes?

   A. One month

   B. One day

   C. No minimum

   D. One billing cycle

   ☑ **C.** AWS services incurring billing only for the time they are actually used. There are no minimum periods of time or commitments when you provision a service.

14. Which AWS service would be used by developers for packaging deployment packages for application code?

   A. CodeCommit

   B. CodeDeploy

   C. CodeBuild

   D. CodeCompile

   ☑ **C.** AWS CodeBuild is used for building deployment packages that are ready for implementation.

15. What types of reserved instances are available on AWS? (Choose two.)

   A. Standard

   B. Conforming

   C. Scalable

   D. Convertible

   E. Flexible

   ☑ **A, D.** The two types of reserved instances are standard and convertible, offering up to 72 percent and 54 percent savings over on-demand pricing, respectively.

16. Which AWS service allows you to purchase reserved instances?

   A. S3

   B. EC2

   C. Lightsail

   D. CloudWatch

   ☑ **B.** EC2 allows you to purchase reserve instances to save on later purchases of pricing under on-demand circumstances.

17. Route 53 can dynamically return different answers to DNS queries based on different circumstances within the AWS infrastructure. Which of the following are circumstances that can be configured with Route 53 to give dynamic responses? (Choose two.)

   A. Geographic location

   B. Incoming port

   C. Latency of systems

   D. Size of transfer request

   E. ACL rules

   ☑ **A, C.** Route 53 can dynamically change responses to DNS queries based on the geographic location of the request or the current latency of systems within AWS for the service requested.

18. Three types of load balancing are used under Elastic Load Balancing. Which of the following is not one of the three types?

   A. Application load balancer

   B. Network load balancer

   C. Dynamic load balancer

   D. Classic load balancer

   ☑ **C.** Dynamic load balancer is not one of the three types under the Elastic Load Balancer service. The three types are application load balancer, which focuses typically on web traffic; network load balancer, which is typically used with high volumes of traffic where performance is key; and classic load balancer, which is a legacy type and not used typically with modern applications and systems.

19. As part of an external audit, you need to provide a list of all users and the access they have within your AWS account. Which report from the IAM console would you generate to provide the auditors this information?

   A. Credential report

   B. User report

   C. IAM report

   D. Account audit report

   ☑ **A.** The credential report contains all users and the access they have within your AWS account. It can be produced and downloaded in CSV format from within the IAM console.

20. Which of the following statements best describes Software as a Service?

    A. The cloud customer is responsible for deploying and configuring virtual machines based upon a managed image.

    B. The cloud customer gets access to a fully managed service via subscription versus installed locally.

    C. The cloud customer gives the user a fully managed platform where only the specific software needed by the user is loaded.

    D. The cloud provider establishes a network and virtualization infrastructure where virtual machines are loaded as software for users to configure.

    ☑ **B.** With Software as a Service, the cloud provider offers a fully established and managed application where the user is only responsible for loading their specific data and applying branding specific to them.

21. The data your application hosts has strict regulatory requirements that you must meet. Which component of the AWS infrastructure would you be most focused on when deploying resources?

    A. Availability Zones

    B. Regions

    C. Edge services

    D. VPC

    ☑ **B.** AWS regions are groups of Availability Zones that are geographically located throughout the world. With the selection of a region, you can assure your data is located under specific jurisdictional requirements or meeting specific requirements that restrict where data can be stored.

22. Which of the following technologies would be used as a security protection for data in transit?

    A. VPC

    B. VPN

    C. ACLs

    D. Security groups

    E. TLS

    ☑ **B, E.** For the protection of data in transit, both Transport Layer Security (TLS) and virtual private networks (VPNs) will protect data as it traverses systems and locations.

23. When looking at the AWS Management Console, you are not seeing services that you have provisioned. Which of the following could be a reason why?

    A. You have not paid for them

    B. Your account requires new access keys

   C. You have not selected the correct region

   D. The console does not show reserved instances

   ☑ **C.** Most resources are provisioned by region, and you must select the proper region within the Management Console to see those resources.

24. You have a rule in a security group that allows HTTPS requests into an EC2 instance. Which statement is true about how the security policy applies to responses to the request?

   A. The response will be blocked without a corresponding rule allowing it

   B. A corresponding ACL must be present to allow the response

   C. Security groups automatically have the same rules for inbound and outbound requests

   D. Security groups will automatically allow traffic that is a response to an allowed request, regardless of what the rules specify

   ☑ **D.** Security groups will automatically allow traffic that is in response to a request made by an allowed rule. For example, if an inbound request is allowed to be made, the corresponding reply is allowed to be made as well, regardless of what the outbound rules specifically allow.

25. Savings plans on AWS offer deep discounts over on-demand pricing based on a commitment for future purchase. Which service is not covered by savings plans?

   A. S3

   B. EC2

   C. Lambda

   D. Fargate

   ☑ **A.** Savings plans cover services under compute resources, which includes EC2, Fargate, and Lambda, but does not cover storage services such as S3.

26. The AWS monthly billing allows for the export and downloading of data. Which format is offered to download your billing data?

   A. JSON

   B. XML

   C. QuickBooks

   D. CSV

   ☑ **D.** The AWS monthly bill is able to be downloaded in CSV format for local processing or importing into other reporting, tracking, or accounting applications.

27. AWS Budgets offers a variety of different planning templates to help users track service consumption and charges. Which of the following are types of budget reports offered? (Choose two.)

    A. Usage budgets

    B. Overage budgets

    C. Storage budgets

    D. Savings plans coverage budgets

    E. Virtualization budgets

    ☑ **A, D.** AWS Budgets offers usage budgets and savings coverage budgets as two of the six types of budgets, which also include cost budgets, reserved instances budgets, reserved instances coverage budgets, and savings plans utilization budgets.

28. You need to be able to quickly verify if data objects in AWS are identical across multiple regions in S3. Which type of algorithm would allow you to quickly and easily accomplish this?

    A. Tokenization

    B. Hashing

    C. Obfuscation

    D. Encryption

    ☑ **B.** Hashing involves taking data of arbitrary type, length, or size and using a function to map a value that is of a fixed size. Hashing can be applied to virtually any type of data object, from text strings, documents, images, binary data, and even virtual machine images. If data objects are identical, they will have the same resulting hash value.

29. You want to run a dynamic website in AWS but do not want to be responsible for deploying or maintaining any servers or software beyond your own application code. Which of the following AWS services would allow you to accomplish this? (Choose two.)

    A. Lightsail

    B. Lambda

    C. CloudFront

    D. CloudTrail

    E. EC2

    ☑ **B, C.** Lambda allows for the serverless running of application code, and CloudFront is a content delivery network for the hosting of web pages and associated components.

30. AWS OpsWorks provides managed instances of popular automation and configuration tools. Which popular utilities are available within OpsWorks? (Choose two.)

    A. Git

    B. SVN

    C. Puppet

    D. CVS

    E. Chef

    ☑ **C, E.** AWS OpsWorks provides managed instances of Puppet and Chef. Both are well-known and widely used automation and server configuration tools used throughout the IT world. The AWS implementation can be used for configuration automation for EC2 instances within AWS, as well as on-premises instances.

31. AWS offers the ability to download or export many reports within the Management Console that you can then use for local processing or importing into other tools. Which data format is offered to export the data from the Management Console?

    A. CSV

    B. JSON

    C. XML

    D. SQL

    ☑ **A.** Reports in the AWS Management Console are typically available to download or export in CSV format to use for local processing or imported into other tools.

32. You suspect one of your employees has been violating company policy with the use of AWS services under your account for personal use. Which AWS service would be valuable to investigate their activities?

    A. CloudTrail

    B. CloudWatch

    C. CloudAudit

    D. CloudLog

    ☑ **A.** CloudTrail is the AWS service for performing auditing and compliance within your AWS account. It analyzes all logs from all services under your account and provides a history of all activities.

33. Rather than using your on-premises VDI solutions, which AWS service could be leveraged to provide your users the same functionality while removing your need to maintain and support a hardware infrastructure?

   A. AppStream

   B. WorkSpaces

   C. WorkLink

   D. AWS DaaS

   ☑ **B.** Amazon WorkSpaces is a Desktop as a Service (DaaS) implementation that is built, maintained, configured, and secured through AWS as a managed service. WorkSpaces offers both Windows and Linux desktop solutions that can be quickly deployed anywhere throughout the AWS global infrastructure. As many organizations have moved to virtual desktop infrastructure (VDI) solutions, WorkSpaces enables them to offer the same solutions to their users, without the need to actually purchase and maintain the hardware required for VDI infrastructure.

34. Your company wants to split budgets out in multiple ways in order to gain insight into costs by department and projects. Which AWS tool under the Billing Dashboard will allow easy implementation of this?

   A. Cost centers

   B. Cost graphs

   C. Cost categories

   D. Cost codes

   ☑ **C.** Cost categories allow an account to categorize services and costs into granular containers for the purposes of analysis based on your specific needs. Services can be grouped into categories based on projects, departments, initiatives, or any other category that is tracked and important to a user.

35. AWS incorporates a variety of robust security services to counter common types of web attacks. Which type of attack is the AWS Shield service designed to protect against?

   A. Cross-site scripting

   B. SQL injection

   C. Brute force

   D. Distributed Denial of Service

   ☑ **D.** The AWS Shield service constantly monitors for and reacts to Distributed Denial of Service (DDoS) attacks.

36. You need to provide application access to a subset of users to test and verify functionality but do not want them to see production data. What type of data deidentification process would you use for this?

    A. Static masking

    B. Dynamic masking

    C. PII masking

    D. Sensitivity masking

    ☑ **B.** With dynamic masking, production environments are protected by the masking process being implemented between the application and data layers of the application. This allows for a masking translation to take place live in the system and during normal application processing of data.

37. What is the easiest method to implement encryption at rest within S3 from the perspective of the user?

    A. Client-side encryption using keys generated by AWS

    B. Server-side encryption using your own keys

    C. Server-side encryption using keys generated by AWS

    D. Client-side encryption using your own keys

    ☑ **C.** With server-side encryption, S3 will automatically encrypt data objects that you upload before they are stored and will decrypt them when accessed and pass the data back to you.

38. With consolidated billing you can merge multiple accounts into a single bill and leverage the combined resources for discounts on AWS services. Which of the following is not a cost that receives discounts under consolidated billing?

    A. EC2

    B. Support plans

    C. Lambda

    D. Fargate

    ☑ **B.** While many AWS services offer volume discounts through consolidated billing, AWS support plans are still done at the account level and are not combined across accounts with consolidated billing.

39. The AWS Marketplace offers images from vendors that are full packages for their products that can be deployed within AWS. Costs for Marketplace offerings have two components. Which of the following are the price components? (Choose two.)

A. S3 costs

B. EC2 costs

C. Support costs

D. Licensing costs

E. Professional services costs

☑ **B, D.** Costs for Marketplace applications will be presented as two costs: the licensing costs from the vendor for use of the image and the EC2 costs for hosting it and the compute/storage resources it will consume.

40. Your company has decided to retire their on-premises data warehouse and move to a similar solution in AWS for increased capacity and lower costs. Which AWS service would you explore for this initiative?

A. Redshift

B. Aurora

C. DynamoDB

D. RDS

☑ **A.** Redshift is a cloud-based data warehouse solution offered by AWS. Unlike traditional on-premises data warehouses, Redshift leverages AWS storage to any capacity that is needed by a company, either now or into the future.

41. Which type of service offerings pushes the responsibility for configuration and operations to AWS and leaves the customer only responsible for loading their data?

A. Unmanaged

B. Regulated

C. Managed

D. Offloaded

☑ **C.** Managed resources are those where the cloud provider is responsible for the installation, patching, maintenance, and security of a resource.

42. When users are created via the IAM console, what can be used to assign granular levels of access within a service?

A. Groups

B. Roles

C. ACLs

D. Settings

☑ **B.** Roles in AWS are the granular permissions that users can be granted. Within each AWS service, there are multiple roles that allow different activities, such as reading data, creating data, deploying services, provisioning access, etc.

43. A system is able to keep functioning when some portions of it experience an outage of resources. What concept refers to this ability?

   A. Availability

   B. Resiliency

   C. Redundancy

   D. Elasticity

   ☑ **B.** Resiliency pertains to the ability of a system to continue to function when some aspects of it experience an outage. This can pertain to overall levels of resources, such as loss of a percentage of capacity, or it can pertain to portions of APIs or storage becoming unavailable.

44. AWS allows for resources to be added to a system without any downtime or interruption to services. What is this concept called?

   A. Elasticity

   B. Scalability

   C. Expandability

   D. Portability

   ☑ **A.** Elasticity allows for resources to be added seamlessly to a system or application without any downtime or interruption to services due to restarts.

45. Which component of AWS Systems Manager provides a consolidated view of data from sources such as CloudTrail and CloudWatch to help with the investigation of operational issues?

   A. Explorer

   B. AppConfig

   C. Systems Manager

   D. OpsCenter

   ☑ **D.** OpsCenter provides a consolidated view for developers and operations staff to view and investigate any operational issues. Data from many different resources, such as CloudTrail logs, CloudWatch alarms, metrics, information about AWS configuration changes, and event and account information, is all centralized. It allows for a quick view of your entire environment and helps diagnosis problems as quickly as possible.

46. Security groups and access control lists (ACLs) are two means of applying security rules within AWS. Which of the following statements is true?

A. Security groups and ACLs can both be applied to subnets and instances

B. Security groups apply to instances; ACLs apply to subnets

C. Security groups apply to subnets; ACLs apply to instances

D. Security groups and ACLs are only used on subnets

☑ **B.** Security groups are rules that are applied to specific instances, while ACLs are applied to subnets.

47. To help manage versioning in AWS S3, the service provides automation tools, called actions, to handle how versions are stored and when they are removed from the system. Which of the following are the types of actions available? (Choose two.)

A. Archive

B. Transition

C. Delete

D. Rotate

E. Expire

☑ **B, E.** S3 actions have both transition and expire types. Transition will move S3 objects to a different storage class after they reach a certain date, and expire will automatically remove objects after they reach a certain age.

48. Under the AWS Shared Responsibility Model and an IaaS implementation, which of the following areas of responsibility reside with the customer? (Choose two.)

A. Application code

B. Operating system

C. Virtualization

D. Storage

E. Networking

☑ **A, B.** Under the AWS Shared Responsibility Model, with an IaaS implementation, both the application code and operating system are the responsibility of the customer.

49. The use of multifactor authentication is imperative to protect accounts with administrative access, especially the root user for your AWS account. Along with a password, which of the following could be used to fulfill multifactor requirements?

A. PIN

B. Question/answer challenge

C. One-time use code

D. Date of birth

☑ **C.** To fulfill multifactor authentication requirements, you must use at least two different categories from something the user knows, something the user has, and something the user is. A one-time code, from either a device, application, or received via text message, would fulfill being something the user has. A PIN, date of birth, or a question/answer challenge all fall into the same category as a password, something the user knows.

50. Rather than creating accounts with passwords in AWS, your corporate policies require you to use your internal credentials via federation with AWS. Which technology could you use to establish federated authentication with AWS?

A. JSON

B. HTTPS

C. RADIUS

D. SAML

☑ **D.** The Security Assertion Markup Language (SAML) facilitates federated login between a local identity provider and a service provider (application) and allows for the secure passing of attributes and trust of external authentication.

51. When adding new users in IAM, you want to be able to assign a set of capabilities to them and keep them uniform between those users. Which feature of IAM would you use to accomplish this?

A. Groups

B. Labels

C. Roles

D. Sets

☑ **A.** Groups are used to assign a standard set of permissions and roles to users as they are added to the system and maintain uniformity between members of the group.

52. Which core concept of cloud computing most relates to the cost-savings benefits you can realize through AWS offerings?

A. Broad network access

B. On-demand self-service

C. Metered service

D. Resource pooling

☑ **C.** Through metered service, you only pay for resources that you are actually using and only during the time when you are actually using them. This concept encapsulates the largest costs savings you can realize through AWS.

53. Which AWS support plan is the lowest level that gives 24/7 access to support?

    A. Free

    B. Business

    C. Enterprise

    D. Developer

    ☑ **B.** The business support plan is designed for those running production workloads within AWS and is the lowest plan that offers 24/7 access to AWS support services.

54. Your company has decided for the first time to start using AWS services for storage. As a precondition, your CEO has demanded assurances that you can quickly remove data from AWS should the need arise. Which core concept of cloud computing would this pertain to?

    A. Portability

    B. Reversibility

    C. Interoperability

    D. Removability

    ☑ **B.** Reversibility is the ability of a cloud customer to take all their systems and data out of a cloud provider and have assurances from the cloud provider that all the data has been securely and completely removed within an agreed-upon timeline.

55. The Trust Advisor can flag AWS services that you have provisioned but are inactive or being used below the level for which they are configured. Which area of Trust Advisor would you explore to find this report?

    A. Performance

    B. Service limits

    C. Cost optimization

    D. Security

    ☑ **C.** The Cost Optimization area flags any resources that you have allocated and are incurring billing and are either not being used at the level they are allocated or are allocated but inactive. This enables users to eliminate resources that are incurring billing and wasting money.

56. You want to do a compliance check with your configurations against best practices. Which AWS service would you use to accomplish this?

    A. Trusted Advisor

    B. IAM dashboard

    C. AWS Management Console

    D. AWS System Manager

☑ **A.** The AWS Trusted Advisor will give a report on compliance with best practices for configurations across your AWS provisioned services.

57. You need to offer easy access to your AWS systems from anywhere, but you do not want to deal with many of the problems of BYOD and the security issues associated with it. Which AWS service would you investigate to accomplish this?

    A. OpsWorks

    B. Lambda

    C. Aurora

    D. WorkSpaces

    ☑ **D.** AWS WorkSpaces offers a Desktop as a Service offering that is fully maintained and managed by AWS but can be accessed by your users from anywhere.

58. When using the AWS Virtual Private Cloud to span between AWS resources and your on-premises resources, what type of cloud deployment are you using?

    A. Public

    B. Community

    C. Private

    D. Hybrid

    ☑ **D.** When spanning between a traditional data center and AWS using a VPC, you are using a hybrid cloud deployment model.

59. Which concept of cloud computing refers to the ability of a system to easily move between different cloud providers?

    A. Interoperability

    B. Portability

    C. Moveability

    D. Transferability

    ☑ **B.** Portability refers to the ability of moving a system easily and seamlessly between cloud providers.

60. Which AWS database service does not use SQL and is highly optimized for key-value data storage?

    A. DynamoDB

    B. Aurora

    C. Redshift

    D. CloudFront

    ☑ **A.** DynamoDB is the AWS key-value and document database solution for those applications that do not need a SQL or relational database but do need extremely high performance and scalable access to their data.

61. Which component of the AWS Management Console allows a user to access the shell and CLI for managing EC2 instances without the use of keys or exposing ports?

    A. Run command

    B. Distributor

    C. Systems Manager

    D. Automation

    ☑ **C.** AWS Systems Manager allows for accessing shell and CLI for managing EC2 instances via a browser and without needing to use keys or expose ports from systems

62. An academic institution has a suite of software packages that it wants to make available to students but does not want to distribute software or be responsible for the support of it on student devices. Which AWS service would be the easiest and most cost-effective means to accomplish this?

    A. WorkSpaces

    B. AppStream

    C. WorkLink

    D. VirtualApp

    ☑ **B.** AppStream is a service for providing managed and streaming applications via AWS. By streaming applications, the need to download and install applications is removed, as they will be run through a web browser. This eliminates the need for an organization to distribute software and support the installation and configuration of it to their users.

63. Which AWS security service would allow you to apply processing rules to web traffic based upon the contents or type of request?

    A. AWS Shield

    B. Route 53

    C. AWS WAF

    D. AWS Inspector

    ☑ **C.** The AWS Web Application Firewall (WAF) monitors and protects against web exploits and attacks based on rules that inspect traffic and requests.

64. Which AWS storage service is used by EC2 instances for high-throughput data operations?

    A. S3

    B. AWS Storage Gateway

    C. Elastic Block Storage

    D. AWS Snow

    ☑ **C.** Amazon Elastic Block Storage (EBS) is high-performance block storage that is used in conjunction with EC2 where high-throughput data operations are required. This will typically include file systems, media services, and both relational and nonrelational databases.

65. You want to use a set of configurations within your code that will use the same key value on all systems but have different values based upon the specific system. Which AWS tool allows you to do this?

    A. Parameter store

    B. State manager

    C. Distributor

    D. Automation

    ☑ **A.** The parameter store provides a way to store configuration data for your applications. This can be either plain-text strings or passwords used to access services such as databases. A main benefit of the parameter store is the ability to use the same key but contain different values for systems. For example, you could have a hostname for a database or API call that gets a different value for systems that are flagged as development, test, or production but allows your code to remain the same throughout.

About the Online Content

This book comes complete with TotalTester Online customizable practice exam software with 130 practice exam questions.

System Requirements

The current and previous major versions of the following desktop browsers are recommended and supported: Chrome, Microsoft Edge, Firefox, and Safari. These browsers update frequently, and sometimes an update may cause compatibility issues with the TotalTester Online or other content hosted on the Training Hub. If you run into a problem using one of these browsers, please try using another until the problem is resolved.

Your Total Seminars Training Hub Account

To get access to the online content, you will need to create an account on the Total Seminars Training Hub. Registration is free, and you will be able to track all your online content using your account. You may also opt in if you wish to receive marketing information from McGraw Hill or Total Seminars, but this is not required for you to gain access to the online content.

Privacy Notice

McGraw Hill values your privacy. Please be sure to read the Privacy Notice available during registration to see how the information you have provided will be used. You may view our Corporate Customer Privacy Policy by visiting the McGraw Hill Privacy Center. Visit the **mheducation.com** site and click **Privacy** at the bottom of the page.

Single User License Terms and Conditions

Online access to the digital content included with this book is governed by the McGraw Hill License Agreement outlined next. By using this digital content you agree to the terms of that license.

Access   To register and activate your Total Seminars Training Hub account, simply follow these easy steps.

1. Go to **hub.totalsem.com/mheclaim**

2. To register and create a new Training Hub account, enter your e-mail address, name, and password on the **Register** tab. No further personal information (such as credit card number) is required to create an account.

    If you already have a Total Seminars Training Hub account, enter your email address and password on the **Log in** tab.

3. Enter your Product Key: **hcds-vrxv-ktgw**

4. Click to accept the user license terms.

5. For new users, click the **Register and Claim** button to create your account. For existing users, click the **Log in and Claim** button.

    You will be taken to the Training Hub and have access to the content for this book.

Duration of License   Access to your online content through the Total Seminars Training Hub will expire one year from the date the publisher declares the book out of print.

Your purchase of this McGraw Hill product, including its access code, through a retail store is subject to the refund policy of that store.

The Content is a copyrighted work of McGraw Hill, and McGraw Hill reserves all rights in and to the Content. The Work is © 2021 by McGraw Hill.

Restrictions on Transfer   The user is receiving only a limited right to use the Content for the user's own internal and personal use, dependent on purchase and continued ownership of this book. The user may not reproduce, forward, modify, create derivative works based upon, transmit, distribute, disseminate, sell, publish, or sublicense the Content or in any way commingle the Content with other third-party content without McGraw Hill's consent.

Limited Warranty   The McGraw Hill Content is provided on an "as is" basis. Neither McGraw Hill nor its licensors make any guarantees or warranties of any kind, either express or implied, including, but not limited to, implied warranties of merchantability or fitness for a particular purpose or use as to any McGraw Hill Content or the information therein or any warranties as to the accuracy, completeness, correctness, or results to be obtained from, accessing or using the McGraw Hill Content, or any material referenced in such Content or any information entered into licensee's product by users or other persons and/or any material available on or that can be accessed through the licensee's product (including via any hyperlink or otherwise) or as to non-infringement of third-party rights. Any warranties of any kind, whether express or implied, are disclaimed. Any material or data obtained through use of the McGraw Hill Content is at your own discretion and risk and user understands that it will be solely responsible for any resulting damage to its computer system or loss of data.

Neither McGraw Hill nor its licensors shall be liable to any subscriber or to any user or anyone else for any inaccuracy, delay, interruption in service, error or omission, regardless of cause, or for any damage resulting therefrom.

In no event will McGraw Hill or its licensors be liable for any indirect, special or consequential damages, including but not limited to, lost time, lost money, lost profits or good will, whether in contract, tort, strict liability or otherwise, and whether or not such damages are foreseen or unforeseen with respect to any use of the McGraw Hill Content.

TotalTester Online

TotalTester Online provides you with a simulation of the AWS Certified Cloud Practitioner (CLF-C01) exam. Exams can be taken in Practice Mode or Exam Mode. Practice Mode provides an assistance window with hints, references to the book, explanations of the correct and incorrect answers, and the option to check your answer as you take the test. Exam Mode provides a simulation of the actual exam. The number of questions, the types of questions, and the time allowed are intended to be an accurate representation of the exam environment. The option to customize your quiz allows you to create custom exams from selected domains or chapters, and you can further customize the number of questions and time allowed.

To take a test, follow the instructions provided in the previous section to register and activate your Total Seminars Training Hub account. When you register, you will be taken to the Total Seminars Training Hub. From the Training Hub Home page, select **AWS Certified Cloud Practitioner All-in-One (Exam CLF-C01) TotalTester** from the Study drop-down menu at the top of the page, or from the list of Your Topics on the Home page. You can then select the option to customize your quiz and begin testing yourself in Practice Mode or Exam Mode. All exams provide an overall grade and a grade broken down by domain.

Technical Support

For questions regarding the TotalTester or operation of the Training Hub, visit **www.totalsem.com** or e-mail **support@totalsem.com**.

For questions regarding book content, visit **www.mheducation.com/customerservice**.

ACLs   Access control list (ACLs) are security layers on the VPC that control traffic at the subnet level. This differs from security groups that are on each specific instance.

alarms   Used within CloudWatch for automation of actions based on defined thresholds or through the use of machine learning algorithms that are designed to spot anomalies. They can trigger actions such as auto-scaling or triggering workflows.

anomaly detection   Anomaly detection is a new machine learning service that analyzes the metrics of systems and applications to determine normal baselines and surface anomalies. The service will send individual reports when an anomaly is detected and will analyze the cause of the anomaly to isolate it to an account, region, or type of usage. You can view results in a chart within the AWS Management Console and also fire CloudWatch alarms.

AppStream   AppStream is a service for providing managed and streaming applications via AWS. By streaming applications, the need to download and install applications is removed, as they will be run through a web browser. This eliminates the need for an organization to distribute software and support the installation and configuration of it to their users.

Aurora   Aurora is an AWS database service, a subset of Amazon RDS, that is compatible with both MySQL and PostgreSQL databases. It is built on MySQL and optimized to use cloud services, such as automatically expanding to meet storage requirements as data is added.

Availability Zones   An Availability Zone (AZ) is one or more data centers with redundant power, networking, and connectivity in an AWS region.

AWS Backup   AWS Backup provides backup services for all AWS services. It provides a single resource to configure backup policies and monitor their usage and success across any services that you have allocated. This allows administrators to access a single location for all backup services without having to separately configure and monitor them on a per-service basis across AWS.

AWS CLI   The AWS Command Line Interface (CLI) provides a way to manage AWS services and perform many administrative functions without having to use the web-based Management Console.

AWS IQ   An AWS service to connect users with AWS Certified freelancers and consulting firms to provide support, consulting, and assistance with AWS services.

AWS Management Console   The main resource where you can control all of your AWS services and perform any operations against them.

AWS Professional Services   The Professional Services group operates mostly based on a series of "offerings," which are a set of activities, documentation, and best practices that form a methodology for customers moving to the cloud. They are designed as a blueprint to quickly achieve outcomes and allow customers to finish projects and offer high reliability of outcomes.

AWS Shield   AWS Shield provides protection from and mitigation of Distributed Denial of Service (DDoS) attacks on AWS services. It is always active and monitoring AWS services, providing continual coverage without needing to engage AWS support for assistance should an attack occur.

AWS WAF   AWS WAF is a web application firewall that protects web applications against many common attacks. AWS WAF comes with an array of preconfigured rules from AWS that will offer comprehensive protection based on common top security risks, but you also have the ability to create your own rules. The AWS WAF includes an API that can be used to automate rule creation and deployment of rules to your allocated resources.

Billing Dashboard   The AWS Billing Dashboard provides you with all the tools you need to view your bills, monitor your usage and costs, and set up consolidated billing for multiple accounts.

block storage   Storage that acts as an individual hard drive and stores chunks of data that are presented to users and applications in a file system structure of directories and files.

budgets   Budgets are used to plan the consumption of services, costs of services, and the use of instance reservations. They can be used to track how close you are to using a budgeted amount of money, as well as the use of the Free Tier. This also includes your usage during a specified time period, including your usage of reservation instances, as well as how much of your overall budget has been used. During each month, budgets will track how much your current charged status is, including what your predicted amount of usage and charges will be by the end of the month.

budget reports   Reports generated on your budgets on either a daily, weekly, or monthly frequency and sent via e-mail to up to 50 addresses.

cloud application   An application that does not reside or run on a user's device, but rather is accessible via a network.

cloud application portability   The ability to migrate a cloud application from one cloud provider to another.

cloud computing Network-accessible platform that delivers services from a large and scalable pool of systems, rather than dedicated physical hardware and more static configurations.

cloud data portability The ability to move data between cloud providers.

cloud deployment model How cloud computing is delivered through a set of particular configurations and features of virtual resources. The cloud deployment models are public, private, hybrid, and community.

CloudFormation CloudFormation implements an automated way to model infrastructure and resources within AWS via either a text file or through the use of programming languages. This allows administrators to build out templates for the provisioning of resources that can then be repeated in a secure and reliable manner

CloudFront Amazon CloudFront is a content delivery network (CDN) that allows for delivery of data and media to users with the lowest levels of latency and the highest levels of transfer speeds. This is done by having CloudFront systems distributed across the entire AWS global infrastructure and fully integrated with many AWS services, such as S3, EC2, and Elastic Load Balancing.

CloudTrail CloudTrail is the AWS service for performing auditing and compliance within your AWS account. CloudTrail pairs with CloudWatch to analyze all the logs and data collected from the services within your account, which can then be audited and monitored for all activities done by users and admins within your account.

CloudWatch CloudWatch is the AWS service for monitoring and measuring services running within the AWS environment. It provides data and insights on application performance and how it may change over time, monitors resource utilization, and provides a centralized and consolidated view of the overall health of systems and services.

CodeBuild AWS CodeBuild is a fully featured code-building service that will compile and test code, as well as build deployment packages that are ready for implementation.

CodeCommit AWS CodeCommit is an AWS-managed service for secure Git repositories.

CodeDeploy AWS CodeDeploy is a managed deployment service that can deploy code to AWS services or on-premises servers.

consolidated billing If you have multiple accounts in AWS, you can opt to consolidate your billing into a single monthly bill, rather than receiving separate bills for each account. With consolidated billing, even though you will only receive one bill, it will still be broken down by individual accounts for tracking purposes and auditing. The great benefit of consolidated billing is the ability to share volume discounts, reserved instance discounts, and savings plans across all of your accounts, rather than each account having its own bill.

container A single system instance that can host multiple virtual environments within it while leveraging the underlying infrastructure.

cost allocation tags   Cost allocation tags are metadata assigned to AWS resources in the form of a key and a value. These can be used to allow an account to quickly track costs associated with resources through very granular views. Cost allocation tags are either generated automatically by AWS or are created by users. The AWS tags will contain information of a system nature, such as created dates, created by what user, region, etc. User tags are defined by the user based on their organization and can include items like project, stack, team, cost center, etc.

cost categories   Cost categories allow an account to categorize services and costs into granular containers for the purposes of analysis based on your specific needs. Services can be grouped into categories based on projects, departments, initiatives, or any other category that is tracked and important to a user. This also allows services to appear in multiple cost categories

Cost Explorer   Cost Explorer allows you to view and analyze both your costs and usage of AWS services. Cost Explorer will display data for 12 months of usage, as well as provide forecasts for what you may use in the next 12 months based on your past usage.

Database Migration Service   The AWS Database Migration Service (DMS) is a tool for migrating data into AWS databases from existing databases with minimal downtime or other interruptions. The DMS can move data from most of the popular and widely used databases into the various AWS database services while the source system remains fully operational.

data at rest (DAR)   Data stored in a database or file system, such as volumes (EBS), S3 objects, and backups.

data in transit (DIT)   Data that flows over a networked connection, either through public unsecured networks or internal protected corporate networks.

data in use (DIU)   Data within a system or application that is currently being processed or is in use, either through the computing resources or residing in memory.

data loss prevention (DLP)   An overall strategy and process for ensuring that users cannot send sensitive or protected information outside of networks or systems that are secured and protected. This can be related to the intentional attempt by users to transfer such information, but it also applies to preventing the accidental sending or leakage of data.

data portability   The ability to move data from one system or another without having to re-enter it.

data warehouse   A centralized repository of historical data from throughout an enterprise that is used for querying and creating reports to be used for business intelligence or data mining.

DynamoDB   DynamoDB is the AWS key/value and document database solution for those applications that do not need a SQL or relational database but do need extremely high performance and scalable access to their data.

EC2   Amazon Elastic Compute Cloud (EC2) is the main offering for virtual servers in the cloud. It allows users to create and deploy compute instances that they will retain full control over and offers a variety of configuration options for resources.

EC2 instance types   EC2 instance types are where the underlying hardware resources are married with the type of image you are using. The instance type will dictate the type of CPU used, how many virtual CPUs (vCPUs) it has, how much memory, the type of storage used, network bandwidth, and the underlying EBS bandwidth. Some instance types also have GPUs for greater processing power.

Edge locations   To provide optimal responsiveness for customers, AWS maintains a network of Edge locations throughout the world to provide ultra-low-latency access to data. These locations are geographically dispersed throughout the world to be close to customers and organizations in order to provide the fastest response times. Unlike regular AWS regions and Availability Zones, Edge locations are optimized to perform a narrow set of tasks and duties, allowing them to be optimally tuned and maintained for their intended focus, without being burdened by the full range of AWS services.

Elastic Beanstalk   With Elastic Beanstalk, you chose the application platform that your code is written in, such as Java, Node.js, PHP, or .NET. Once you provision the instance, you can deploy your code into it and begin running. You only select the platform that you need—you do not select specific hardware or compute resources.

Elastic Block Storage   Amazon Elastic Block Storage (EBS) is high-performance block storage that is used in conjunction with EC2 where high-throughput data operations are required. This will typically include file systems, media services, and both relational and nonrelational databases.

Elastic Load Balancing   Elastic Load Balancing is used to distribute traffic across the AWS infrastructure. This can be done with varying degrees of granularity, ranging from spanning across multiple Availability Zones or within a single Availability Zone. It is focused on fault tolerance by implementing high availability, security, and auto-scaling capabilities. There are three different types of load balancing under its umbrella: application load balancer, network load balancer, and classic load balancer.

Elasticity   The ability of a cloud environment to dynamically change the level of resources allocated to a system or application based on changing needs and in real time. This will include adjusting resources for applications where sudden or unexpected demands are mitigated by adding additional capacity and then automatically releasing resources when no longer needed

Free Tier   Services that are free to use for AWS users that can be either permanent, for 12 months, or on a trial basis.

Glacier   S3 Glacier is a special type of S3 storage that is intended to be a secure solution for long-term data archiving and backups.

Glacier Deep   S3 Glacier Deep is a subset of Glacier for even longer-term storage that allows cost savings based upon longer retrieval times.

groups (within Billing)   Used to organize AWS services for use in the Billing Dashboard for budgets, cost estimates, and other reporting.

hashing   Hashing involves taking data of an arbitrary type, length, or size and using a mathematical function to map the data to a value that is of a fixed size. Hashing can be applied to virtually any type of data object, from text strings, documents, images, binary data, and even virtual machine images.

IAM dashboard   The AWS Identity and Access Management dashboard where user accounts can be created and security applied to them for access to your AWS account, as well as creating, editing, or deleting users, roles, groups, policies, and more.

Infrastructure as a Service (IaaS)   The capability provided to a consumer to provision processing, storage, networks, and other fundamental computing resources in order to deploy and run arbitrary software, including operating systems and applications. The consumer does not manage or control the underlying cloud infrastructure, but has control over operating systems, storage, and deployed applications—and possibly limited control of select networking components such as host firewalls.

interoperability   The ease and ability to reuse components of a system or application, regardless of underlying system design and provider.

key management service (KMS)   A system or service that manages keys used for encryption within a system or application that is separate from the actual host system. The KMS will typically generate, secure, and validate keys.

Knowledge Center   An FAQ page that is maintained by AWS Services and addresses the most common types of issues and support questions from AWS users.

Lambda   AWS Lambda is a service for running code for virtually any application or back-end service. All you need to do is upload your code, and there are no systems or resources to manage.

Lightsail   Lightsail is the quickest way to get into AWS for new users. It offers blueprints that will configure fully ready systems and application stacks for you to immediately begin using and deploy your code or data into. Lightsail is fully managed by AWS and is designed to be a one-click deployment model to get you up and running quickly at a low cost.

Machine Images   Amazon Machine Images (AMIs) are the basis of virtual compute instances in AWS. An image is basically a data object that is a bootable virtual machine and can be deployed throughout the AWS infrastructure. AMIs can be either those offered by AWS though their Quick Start options, those offered by vendors through the AWS Marketplace, or those created by users for their own specific needs.

managed resources   Resources where the cloud provider is responsible for the installation, patching, maintenance, and security.

measured service   Cloud services are delivered and billed for in a metered way.

multitenancy   Having multiple customers and applications running within the same environment but in a way that they are isolated from each other and not visible to each other but share the same resources.

object storage   Storage where data is a distinct object and called by a unique identifier rather than being organized in a file system structure with folders.

on-demand self-service   A cloud customer can provision services in an automatic manner, when needed, with minimal involvement from the cloud provider.

OpsWorks   AWS OpsWorks provides managed instances of Puppet and Chef.

Platform as a Service (PaaS)   The capability provided to the customer to deploy into the cloud a platform to host consumer-created or acquired applications written using programming languages, libraries, services, and tools supported by the provider. The customer does not manage or control the underlying cloud infrastructure, including the network, servers, operating systems, and storage, but has control over the deployed applications and possibly configuration settings for the application-hosting environment.

portability   The ability for a system or application to seamlessly and easily move between different cloud providers.

Pricing Calculator   The AWS Pricing Calculator services as your one-stop shop for generating estimates for all AWS services. It can be used for a single estimate for one service or can be used to add an entire menu of services to generate a consolidated estimate.

Redshift   Redshift is a cloud-based data warehouse solution offered by AWS. Unlike traditional on-premises data warehouses, Redshift leverages AWS storage to any capacity that is needed by a company, either now or in the future

regions   AWS organizes resources throughout the world in regions. Each region is a group of logical data centers, called Availability Zones. While each region may seem like it is a data center or a physical location, it is actually a collection of independent data centers that are grouped and clustered together, providing redundancy and fault tolerance.

Relational Database Service   Amazon Relational Database Service (RDS) is an umbrella service that incorporates several different kinds of database systems. Each system is fully managed by AWS and is optimized within the AWS infrastructure for memory, performance, and I/O. All aspects of the database management, such as provisioning, configuration, maintenance, performance monitoring, and backups, are handled by AWS.

reserved instances   AWS allows users to pre-purchase resources and capacity for AWS EC2 services. These are based upon a one- or three-year commitment and can offer up to a 72 percent discount against the prices you would normally be charged when resources are allocated on-demand. Reserved instances are based upon specific Availability Zones and match specific criteria, such as instance type and specific resources.

resource pooling   The aggregation of resources allocated to cloud customers by the cloud provider.

root account   The master account that controls all aspects of an AWS account and should be protected with the highest level of security.

Route 53   Amazon Route 53 is a robust, scalable, and highly available DNS service. Rather than running their own DNS services or being dependent on another commercial service, an organization can utilize Route 53 to transform names into their IP address, as well as having full IPv6 compatibility and access. Route 53 can be used for services that reside inside AWS, as well as those outside of AWS.

reversibility   The ability of a cloud customer to remove all data and applications from a cloud provider and completely remove all data from their environment.

S3   Amazon Simple Storage Service (S3) is the most prominent and widely used storage service under AWS. It offers object storage at incredibly high-availability levels, with stringent security and backups, and is used for everything from websites, backups, archives, and big data implementations.

savings plans   Savings plans are a pricing model for AWS compute usage that offers up to a 72 percent discount on on-demand pricing by committing to purchasing a set amount of compute power (in $/hour) over a one- or three-year span, similar to reserved instances. Savings plans apply across instance types, size, operation system, or region and also apply to the AWS Fargate and Lambda services.

scalability   The ability for a cloud customer to statistically add or remove allocated resources to meet expected demand or a change in services.

security groups   Security groups in AWS are virtual firewalls that are used to control inbound and outbound traffic. Security groups are applied on the actual instance within a VPC versus at the subnet level.

service quotas   In order to protect the availability for all users in AWS, service quotas (formerly called limits) are applied to each service. These quotas are specific to a region and will place a limit on the number of specific types of resources you can allocate by default.

SOC reports   Audit and accounting reports, focused on an organization's controls, that are employed when providing secure services to users.

Software as a Service (SaaS)   The capability provided to the customer to use the provider's applications running on a cloud infrastructure. The applications are accessible from various client devices through either a thin client interface, such as a web browser (for example, web-based e-mail), or a program interface. The consumer does not manage or control the underlying cloud infrastructure, including the network, servers, operating systems, storage, and even individual application capabilities, with the possible exception of limited user-specific application settings.

Storage Gateway   The AWS Storage Gateway provides storage for hybrid cloud services that gives access to your on-premises resources to the full array of storage services in AWS. This enables a customer to extend their storage capabilities into AWS seamlessly and with very low latency.

Snow   AWS Snow is designed for offering compute and storage capabilities to those organizations or places that are outside the areas where AWS regions and resources operate. Snow is based on hardware devices that contain substantial compute and storage resources that can be used both as devices for data processing away from the cloud and as a means to get data into and out of AWS. This is particularly useful in situations where high-speed or reliable networking is not possible.

subnets   Subnets are logical subdivisions of an IP network that can be used to organize systems or for the application of security rules.

Systems Manager   The AWS Systems Manager allows you to consolidate data from AWS services and automate tasks across all of your services. It allows for a holistic view of all of your AWS services, while also allowing you to create logical groups of resources that can then be viewed in a consolidated manner.

tenant   An entity that occupies resource space. A single-tenant application has only one entity occurring in a resource, versus a multitenant application that has multiple entities occupying the same space, such as a cloud environment where many different entities operate within the same pool of resources.

tokenization   The process of replacing and substituting secured or sensitive data in a data set with an abstract or opaque value that has no use outside of the application.

Trusted Advisor   A dashboard to check whether your account configurations are in compliance with established best practices in the areas of cost optimization, performance, security, fault tolerance, and service limits.

Virtual Private Cloud   With Amazon Virtual Private Cloud (Amazon VPC), you can create a logically defined space within AWS to create an isolated virtual network. Within this network, you retain full control over how the network is defined and allocated. You fully control the IP space, subnets, routing tables, and network gateway settings within your VPC, and you have full use of both IPv4 and IPv6.

WorkLink   WorkLink offers users the ability to access internal applications through the use of mobile devices.

WorkSpaces   Amazon WorkSpaces is a Desktop as a Service (DaaS) implementation that is built, maintained, configured, and secured through an AWS-managed service. WorkSpaces offers both Windows and Linux desktop solutions that can be quickly deployed anywhere throughout the AWS global infrastructure.

INDEX